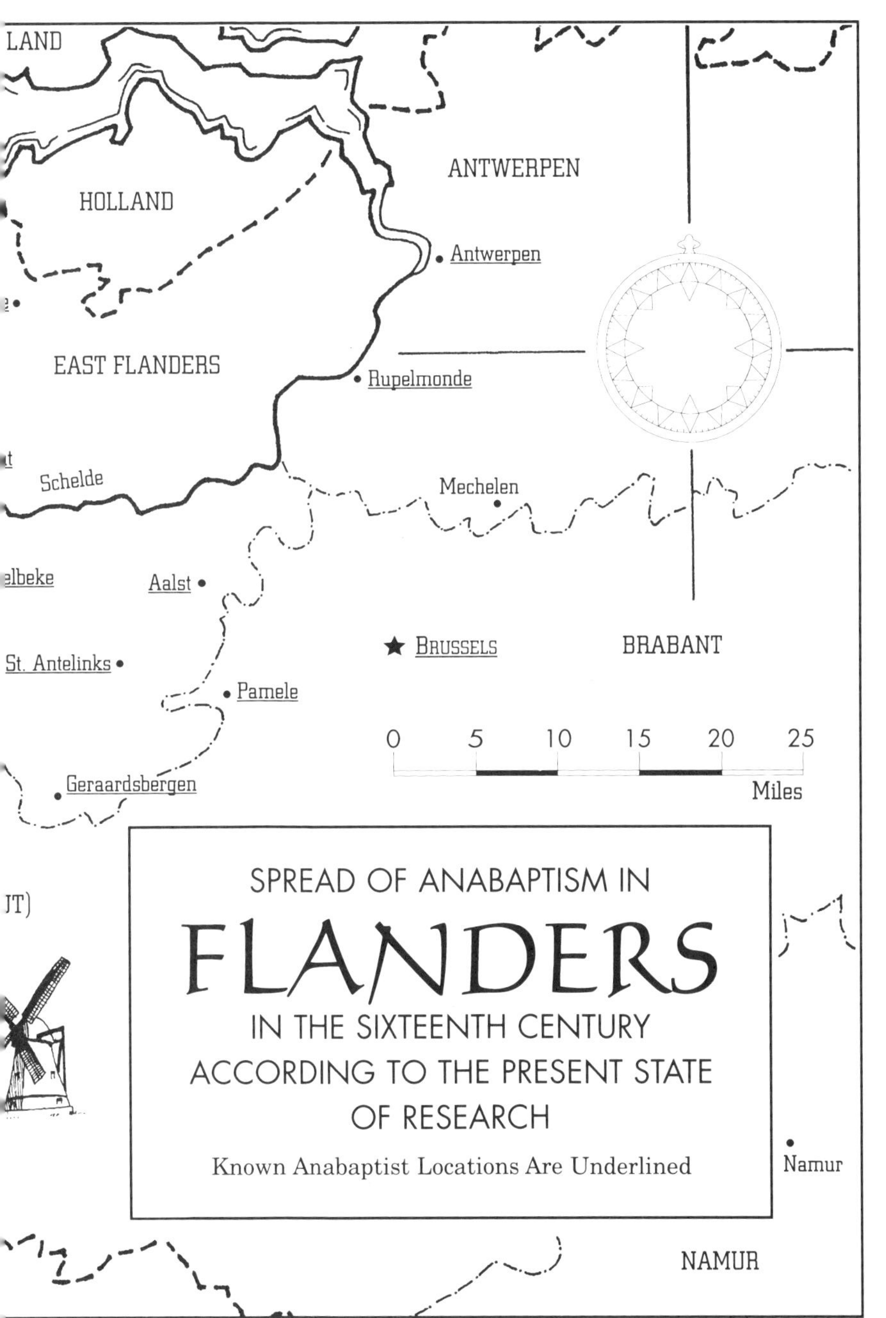

SPREAD OF ANABAPTISM IN

FLANDERS

IN THE SIXTEENTH CENTURY
ACCORDING TO THE PRESENT STATE
OF RESEARCH

Known Anabaptist Locations Are Underlined

"Whom Shall I Fear?"

"Whom Shall I Fear?"

By Kendra Burkholder

Researched and assisted by

Dale Burkholder

Artist: Evelyn Fern Hackman

Cover Artist: Rhoda Horning

ROD AND STAFF PUBLISHERS, INC.

Crockett, Kentucky 41413

Credit:

Map on endsheets taken from *Anabaptism in Flanders* (1961), A.L.E. Verheyden, Herald Press. Used by permission.

Code no. 96-1

In memory of
Claudine
and all faithful martyrs
throughout the ages
who overcame by the blood
of the Lamb
and loved not their lives
unto death

Chapter 1

Claudine scurried about her kitchen, briskly preparing the evening meal. "Margriete, could you please set the table?"

There was a clatter of dishes and spoons as the little girl hurried to do her mother's bidding. At six years old, Margriete was a dependable helper.

Singing softly as she worked, Claudine carried a kettle of steaming soup to the table. She stepped around Pieter and Nicolas, who were playing on the floor. Thankfully, just now they were playing nicely. At times Nicolas, who was just beginning to toddle around, could frustrate his three-year-old brother.

Claudine glanced out the window. Piersom should soon be home from the mill. Yes, there was his familiar figure, striding over the bridge and coming up the street.

As the door swung open, she turned to greet her husband. She had always made it her goal to welcome him home with a smile. "Good evening."

"Hello." Piersom smiled in return and turned to greet the children, who ran to meet him.

Claudine studied her husband across the supper table. He seemed preoccupied this evening. As he ate his supper, he seemed deep in thought, scarcely hearing what anyone said. "Did you have a good day at the mill?" Claudine ventured.

"I was rather busy today," he responded absent-mindedly. Then he lapsed into silence again.

Now Claudine too was unusually quiet as she tended the children and ate her own supper. Finally she asked, "Is something wrong?"

Piersom looked up, startled. "Why?"

"It seems you're extra quiet this evening."

"I heard bad news today. I guess that's been

occupying my mind." Abruptly he paused as his eyes fell on his daughter, who was listening anxiously to his every word. "We'll talk about it later," he told his wife.

Claudine too had noticed Margriete's interest and wished she had not said anything. Margriete had heard too much already. It was the year 1565, and these were troubled times. They had to guard carefully what they said so that they would not frighten the children. Their young minds could not comprehend all that was happening, but what they caught sounded frightening, especially so to Margriete. Lately Margriete's fears and nightmares had caused them to think twice before they discussed the spreading persecution in her presence.

"What did you say, Father?" Margriete wondered.

"It's nothing for you to worry about. God will take care of us." (Once more he must remind her of this.) "It's just something I want to talk with Mother about sometime. Now I want you to tell me what you did today." Thus the conversation returned to safer subjects until the children had been tucked into bed for the night.

After they were alone, Piersom began,

"Claudine, I heard troubling news today. It seems the Inquisitors are getting more determined as the days go by. They have placed five hundred soldiers here in Brugge. The soldiers have one job—to disrupt every meeting we have.

"I'm very concerned about that. But we can't stop meeting together." He sat thinking. As a minister of the church in Brugge, the responsibility weighed heavily upon his shoulders. "The church leaders are meeting together late this evening at the house of Francois van Ieper. Perhaps that will be safer than at one of the ministers' homes, you know."

Claudine understood. Brother Francois was the announcer for the meetings held in their hometown of Brugge.

Piersom walked to the window and looked out. "It's dark outside now. I think I'll go." With that, he said good-bye and was gone.

Claudine was left alone with her thoughts. Ever since she could remember, Pieter Titelman, the well-known and much-dreaded Inquisitor, had been busy hunting "heretics." He had been appointed to find every person who was not loyal to the Catholic state church. Pieter Titelman and his helpers were dreaded by the Christians because of his reputation for being so cruel. He was a man who seemed to have no conscience; his policy was to brutally get rid of any and all who would not submit themselves to his demands.

Claudine's thoughts wandered on. Things would have been much worse for the believers had it not been for one thing. Many people, though they did not join the believers, did not approve of the Inquisition. People everywhere disliked their Spanish king. King Philip ruled over them from a distance, having inherited Flanders from his Flemish father, King Charles V. He did not understand the language, and it seemed he did not understand the people either. Even the town councils, who were supposed to hold trials and sentence those who were arrested by the Spanish Inquisitors, sometimes refused to cooperate.

Claudine recalled how more than one businessman in Brugge had complained to Piersom at the mill. So many people were fleeing from one city to another to escape persecution that it hurt their businesses. They did not like the Inquisition. Piersom could understand their concern, for it affected him too. How could he keep on paying his bills when the price of wheat was steadily rising?

Yesterday in the marketplace, Claudine had seen a poster that some indignant person had nailed up. It was filled with scathing remarks about the Inquisitors and their awful cruelty. Although Claudine knew that none of their brethren would have hung the poster, here again was proof that people were angry about the persecution.

She recalled stories of bolder reactions against the Inquisitors. Once a sympathizer had thrown a stick between a horse's legs in an attempt to hinder an arrest. There were stories too of "negligent" jailers. More than once the bailiffs had refused to stop crowds of hundreds of people who had surrounded a house and blocked the way for an Inquisitor intending to make an arrest.

Of course, Piersom and Claudine could not smile with approval upon these actions. Even though it had at times spared the Christians, it still was not right. Did not the Scriptures teach, "Resist not evil: but whosoever shall smite thee on thy right cheek, turn to him the other also"?[1]

Claudine's heart grew heavy as she thought of the confusion of beliefs around them. How could their faith and testimony be understood when there were so many groups, each standing for something different? There were the Catholics, who were faithful to the state church, as the law commanded everyone to be. Then there were those who could not submit themselves to the Catholic Church. Piersom and Claudine were a part of the group known as Mennists.* They made it their goal to do all that the Scriptures taught and only what they taught.

In addition to the Catholics and the Mennists, there were the Calvinists and the Lutherans, who also refused to be a part of the state church. In some things, they shared similar beliefs with the Mennists, but Piersom and Claudine felt that they could not be a part of these groups, for they were known to fight to protect themselves when the Inquisitors came for them. This was not what the Bible taught, and thus their consciences would not allow it. Nor did the Calvinists and the Lutherans share the belief of the Mennists that the church must be made up of genuine believers only. They, like the Catholics, wanted a church with everyone baptized into it as infants. The Mennists firmly believed that Baptism was only for those who were mature enough to exercise a personal faith

*Mennists derived their name from a prominent leader, Menno Simons, who lived in Holland and died in 1561.

and commitment to Christ as their Lord, and that therefore infant baptism was unscriptural.

What a sad state of confusion. How could they leave a clear witness to those around them? And indeed there were many miserable people who did not enjoy God's peace in their hearts such as the faithful believers did.

Claudine's thoughts turned back to the present. Now what? The situation did not look promising. She knew all too well that, in spite of all the people who sympathized with them, many believers had given their lives in death during the past number of years because they had refused to give up their faith. Would she too face that?

In her heart, she struggled with the question "Do I have a faith strong enough to face torture and death if God should allow it to come to me?" She thought of the little book that had brought her so much inspiration. *Het Offer des Heeren* (*The Offering of the Lord*) contained many examples of faithful martyrs. It told of courageous souls who had died painful deaths at the hands of their persecutors in the years gone before. They had chosen to die rather than to give up their faith.

As Claudine thought of those martyrs and

what they had suffered, fear gripped her heart. How must it feel to be racked, whipped, or burned at the stake? How could anyone endure such terrible pain and suffering? She shuddered to think of it.

As she thought of Piersom and the children, her very being seemed to cry out, "Lord, don't let anything happen to us. We have such a happy family. Just let us live together peacefully. What would our children do without their mother and father? They're so helpless and dependent on us. It would be too much to see them suffer." But countless other mothers and fathers had already faced this very thing. Why should she expect the Lord to spare her?

A knot of anxiety tightened painfully within her breast. She knew she had to come to God and ask His help to overcome her fear and give her His peace in her heart. As she prayed and thought of God's promises, a measure of peace overcame the knot of anxiety. She knew that, whatever the future held for them, God would provide, and He would give strength. After all, He had promised, "I will never leave thee, nor forsake thee"[2] and "My grace is sufficient for thee."[3] She knew that she must simply take one day at a time and trust the future to God.

A sense of weariness stole over her, and she rose from her reverie to prepare for bed. But sleep would not come, as she lay wondering what Piersom would have to say when he returned. She breathed a silent prayer for his safety. At last she heard the sound of the opening door announcing Piersom's return. Soon he was sharing the events of the evening.

"There are indeed many soldiers in the city. I saw two just in the short distance between here and Brother Francois's place. They were strolling along, keeping their eyes open for anything suspicious, I suppose. Makes a person feel a bit uneasy. We talked it over at the meeting, and most everyone feels it is too dangerous to continue meeting here in the city. Some are suggesting that we meet in the Tillegem woods outside the city. It means farther to go for most of us, but I don't think it's impossible. It's barely two miles out of the city."

"But won't they get suspicious if they see so many people going that way?"

"We talked about that too. But it still seems better than trying to meet here in the city. We could go by several different routes and take care not to go in big groups. We decided also to meet at night or at times when the town church is not meeting so it will seem less suspicious."

"When did you plan to meet there?" Claudine asked.

"Tomorrow evening will be the first. I must get up early in the morning so I can get my work at the mill finished in good time. That means," Piersom concluded with a yawn, "we'd better get some sleep."

After kneeling by their bed in heartfelt and earnest prayer for the Lord's protection in the coming days, Claudine and Piersom were soon sound asleep.

Chapter 2

Early the next evening Piersom and Claudine started to the Tillegem woods with their family. The children had taken long naps that afternoon in preparation for their later bedtime. They left early to allow plenty of time for their evening walk. Claudine was thankful for Piersom's strong arms. Nicolas was just learning to walk, and he would not be able to walk such a distance. Even three-year-old Pieter might need to be carried some.

The evening walk was peaceful in the warm sunshine of the summer day, and they reached their destination without incident. Following a trail deep into the woods, they came upon a clearing made by woodcutters. Weary from their journey, the tired family found a comfortable spot and sat down to rest.

Claudine looked about her, awed by the beauty of nature and the wonder of meeting at such a place, alone with God and His people. Out here in the woods away from the town, all seemed so quiet and peaceful; so near to God. This did indeed seem like a good meeting place.

Others were gathering too, coming from various paths in the woods. The familiar greeting, "The peace of the Lord be with you," could be heard among the believers, with the answering response, "Amen,"* followed by the kiss of charity.[4] Piersom had risen from his seat to greet someone whom Claudine did not recognize. She wondered who the stranger might be. Could he perhaps be a visiting minister? This would not be unusual, for some ministers traveled frequently to avoid the danger of becoming too well-known in one place.

Or suppose it was a Judas? Such things had happened before. What if he was pretending to be a believer so that he could betray them? No,

*Cornelius Krahn, *Dutch Anabaptism (Herald Press, 1981), p.184.*

she must not let such worries trouble her. She breathed a prayer for the safety of their meeting tonight, and determined not to worry.

The congregation began to sing softly as a few last ones continued to arrive.

My God, where shall I wend my flight?
    Ah, help me on upon the way;
The foe surrounds both day and night,
    And fain my soul would rend and slay.
Lord God, Thy Spirit give to me;
Then on Thy ways I'll constant be,
And in Life's Book eternally!

When in Egypt I still stuck fast
    And traveled calm, broad paths of ease,
Then was I famed, a much-sought guest;
    The world with me was quite at peace.
Enmeshed was I in Satan's gauze;
My life abomination was;
Right well I served the devil's cause.

But when I turned unto the Lord
    And gave the world a farewell look,
Accepted help against the horde,
    The lore of antichrist forsook,
Then was I mocked and sore defamed,

"Whom Shall I Fear?"

Since Babel's councils I declined;
The righteous man is e'er disclaimed!

As one may read of Abel, famed,
    Zacharias too—recall it well—
Brave Daniel, whom some bad men framed
    So that he among fierce lions fell;
So were the prophets treated, all,
Christ Jesus too—'tis well to recall—
Nor were the apostles spared this call.

I'd rather choose the sorrow sore,
    And suffer as of God the child,
Than have from Pharaoh all his store
    To revel in for one brief while;
The realm of Pharaoh cannot last,
Christ keeps His kingdom sure and fast;
Around His child His arm He casts.**

How special it was to praise God in song. They did not always have this privilege when they were assembled, for a passer-by might hear and report them. But here alone with nature and God, it seemed safe to sing softly. These

**Written by Menno Simons, c. 1514. Used by permission from *The Complete Writings of Menno Simons* (Herald Press, 1956).

believers were worshiping God in spite of the fact that they could pay for it with their lives.

When the last ones had arrived, Piersom took his place at the front of the group. The silent crowd listened expectantly.

"I thank God for the privilege we have to worship God here tonight. With the events of the past week in mind, I want to challenge and encourage you to remain faithful, no matter what the cost. I'm sure you all know by now of the five hundred soldiers stationed here in Brugge. Their presence could mean imprisonment and even death for some of us gathered here tonight. Are we able to stand? No, in our own strength none of us is able. But 'greater is he that is in you, than he that is in the world.'[5]

"To encourage my own faith, I read various portions from the Scriptures this week that speak of persecutions. It was a great inspiration to me, and I want to share these truths with you. In Jesus' Sermon on the Mount, we read, 'Blessed are ye, when men shall revile you, and persecute you, and shall say all manner of evil against you falsely, for my sake. Rejoice, and be exceeding glad: for great is your reward in heaven: for so persecuted they the prophets which were before you.'[6]

"Did you notice that Jesus commands us to be exceeding glad? How can we be exceeding glad when we must suffer? He says we are blessed; I believe we can rejoice because we receive special grace and blessings at such a time, and at the end of our suffering, a great reward awaits us in heaven. Jesus promises us that in these verses."

Claudine's heart was touched with new peace and confidence as she listened to the words of her minister husband. She realized anew that with God on her side, she could face anything. As Piersom spoke at length about a great reward in heaven for those who are faithful, Claudine determined in her heart that with God's help she would be true to the end, no matter what that end might be and what suffering it might bring.

Piersom was now reading from the Book of Peter. Claudine recalled that this morning he had quoted a few of these verses to her. She listened closely to their familiar ring. " 'But and if ye suffer for righteousness' sake, happy are ye: and be not afraid of their terror, neither be troubled; but sanctify the Lord God in your hearts: and be ready always to give an answer to every man that asketh you a reason of the hope that is in you with meekness and fear: having a good conscience; that, whereas they speak evil of you, as of evildoers, they may be ashamed that falsely accuse your good conversation in Christ. For it is better, if the will of God be so, that ye suffer for well doing, than for evil doing.' "[7]

The congregation gathered under the sheltering trees drank in these words eagerly. Here was direction for them in the face of new dangers. Piersom made special note of the fact that, according to these verses, they were not to be troubled or afraid. What a challenge! Could they go about their duties untroubled and unafraid when they never knew what sufferings a new day might bring forth? Yes, Piersom was telling them that God's grace could enable them to do that.

Piersom seemed especially concerned for his congregation gathered around him. He pointed out that they must always be ready to speak about their faith, as this Scripture commanded. "We are *always* to be ready to give an answer to *every* man that asks us the reason for our hope, be it the magistrate or the judge or a neighbor. We need to know the Scriptures well so that we will have an answer for our critics, should we be brought to trial for our faith."

When Piersom had finished his message, he announced the presence of a visiting brother who also had a message for them.

With no further introduction, the stranger whom Claudine had seen earlier took his place at the front. So he was a visiting minister, as she had suspected. She studied the tall, brown-bearded man. His humble, sincere manner seemed fitting for a leader.

He greeted them warmly. "I'm happy to be with you, my fellow believers and citizens of a heavenly country. It does my heart good to find brethren in other places serving the same God I serve. May God keep all of you in His care in the coming days.

"I have received news recently that weighs heavily upon my heart. I'm sure many of you remember the minister Joachim Vermeerem, who traveled in these parts some years ago. It is likely that some of you may even have been baptized by him."

Some affirmative nods were seen here and there as the congregation waited anxiously to hear what the troubling news would be.

"Joachim has been imprisoned for some time now over in Cologne. There they are not so quick to put believers to death. They try long and hard to dissuade them. I recently learned that he has recanted."

What depressing news for these Christians gathered together in hiding! A leader, a shepherd, one who had guided some of them at times! How could he turn his back on his faith? Some heads were shaking sadly. Could it be?

"So, little flock, the message upon my heart this day is for us all, leaders included. The Scriptures tell us, 'Let him that thinketh he standeth take heed lest he fall.'[8] None of us is so strong that he cannot fall in the midst of temptation. We are weak, and need daily to call upon God for strength.

"We live in dangerous times indeed. I do not say this because of the soldiers and the prisons, but I am thinking now of the many false teachers who would try to sway us from the truth. Brethren, stand fast in the faith. As the Scriptures say, 'Put on the whole armour of God, that ye may be able to stand against the wiles of the devil. For we wrestle not against flesh and blood, but against principalities, against powers, against the rulers of the darkness of this world, against spiritual wickedness in high places. Wherefore take unto you the whole armour of God, that ye may be able to withstand in the evil day, and having done all, to stand. Stand therefore, having your loins girt about with truth, and having on the breastplate of righteousness; and your feet shod with the preparation of the gospel of peace.' "[9]

Although they had been listening for some time, the group of hearers did not grow weary. They eagerly drank in the admonitions and instructions on how to be armored so as to be able to stand against the devil's temptations.

The speaker went on to warn of the many false teachers about them. They knew of whom he was speaking. There were others also who disagreed with the state church, such as the Calvinists and the Lutherans. "We must follow the Scriptures and make sure we follow them all. Remember that Jesus said, 'My kingdom is not of this world: if my kingdom were of this world, then would my servants fight.'[10] Thus we cannot take up the sword to protect ourselves as some others do.

"It becomes difficult for our faith to be understood by those looking on when so many different churches have different and opposing practices. My brethren, the devil loves to have it so. And he will seek to turn us from the truth as well. That is why I wish to encourage you to study the Scriptures and be very careful to follow all the truths found there.

"We dare not be a part of the state church, even if it costs us our lives. We have been commanded in the Bible to 'flee from idolatry.'[11] We cannot reverence those images. We have been commanded to 'repent, and be baptized . . . in the name of Jesus Christ for the remission of sins.'[12] We cannot continue to have our babies baptized when they are yet innocent and cannot repent.

"Also we have been clearly commanded, 'Be ye not unequally yoked together with unbelievers: for what fellowship hath righteousness with unrighteousness? and what communion hath light with darkness? and what concord hath Christ with Belial? or what part hath he that believeth with an infidel? and what agreement hath the temple of God with idols? For ye are the temple of the living God; as God hath said, I will dwell in them, and walk in them; and I will be their God, and they shall be my people. Wherefore come out from among them, and be ye separate, saith the Lord, and touch not the unclean thing; and I will receive you, and will be a Father unto you, and ye shall be my sons and daughters, saith the Lord Almighty.'[13] Need we any clearer teaching than we have here?

"This teaching is consolation to me that we are doing the right thing by separating ourselves from the wrongs of the state church. If we keep ourselves pure from wrong, God has promised to dwell in our hearts and be a Father to us. What more do we need?"

Claudine was thankful for the strength she received, and her conviction was intensified that they had chosen the right way. How wonderful it was to be here with the brethren. Because of her little children, she knew it would not always be possible for her to come to the meetings here in the woods, so she drank in every word eagerly.

As the service drew to a close, the sun had sunk below the horizon, deepening the shadows in the woods. It was time to start for home.

Claudine and Piersom talked quietly as they walked along with their family. "The messages this evening were fitting for our times. They gave me new courage," Claudine said.

"God be praised," answered Piersom. "I suppose you didn't know the man who spoke to us, did you?"

"No, I didn't. Who was he?"

"He is Brother Pauwels van Meenen, a leader from the churches in southern Flanders. I felt it would be safer not to introduce him."

"Piersom, how could Brother Joachim give up his faith? That frightens me. If a leader and baptizer gives up, how can any of us stand?"

"I know it's troubling, Claudine. We must depend on God's grace to keep us. If we rely on our own strength, we won't stand." He paused, lost in thought, and then went on. "Torture would be an awful thing to face. But God is able to keep us from falling; I'm sure of that. I know I haven't been tested yet, and maybe my time will come; I don't know. But just think—can you imagine how he feels right now? Surely he has to be a troubled man. How can he be happy and at peace since he has gone back to again embrace all those things that are so wrong? Can he look forward to a reward in heaven?"

"I hadn't thought much about how he must be feeling. Oh, the poor, miserable man. We must pray for him. It would be far better to suffer a cruel death than to go on living without the peace of God's blessing on your life. May God keep me from ever doing such a thing."

"And me also," echoed Piersom.

They walked on, each busy with his own thoughts. Claudine's mind had wandered back to when she had once before heard of a leader who had turned his back on the true faith in order to escape persecution. She now recalled how that incident had troubled her.

She and Piersom had just been married at the time. For them, life lay before them like a clean page. They wanted it to remain unmarred by anything. Dedicated to each other, they shared fond dreams of a happy, peaceful life together.

Claudine recalled how she and Piersom had often talked about the ever-increasing unrest and dissatisfaction with the state church. Why were so many people leaving the state church when they knew it would only bring them trouble and suffering? Who was right? The longer they had wondered, the more unsettled they had become.

Then they began to puzzle over some of the accepted practices of the Catholic Church. Should babies be baptized? Did that make them good adults? What about all the people in the church, some priests included, who lived very wicked and immoral lives? Would a dead saint actually hear their prayers and send them aid as they had been taught to believe? Did God have pleasure in the images before which they prayed? Could forgiveness really be found for their sins by confessing them to the priest? And how could the bread they were given at Mass actually be Jesus' real flesh, as they had been told?

These doubts continued to plague them more and more as the unrest around them grew. Claudine could remember the void that seemed to fill her life. What was missing? Surely there was more to life than the endless cycle of sinning, confessing to the priest, doing penance, and sinning again. Where should they turn?

Piersom could read, and he began to search the Scriptures. Nowhere could he find that babies should be baptized. Instead, he read that a person must repent and be baptized. How could an infant repent? First Timothy 2:5 said, "For there is one God, and one mediator between God and men, the man Christ Jesus." Why did it not mention the priests? Acts 17 read, "Neither is [God] worshipped with men's hands, as though he needed any thing. . . . We ought not to think that the Godhead is like unto gold, or silver, or stone, graven by art and man's device." Why then pray before those images?

And the Scriptures said nothing about praying to dead saints. Could these persecuted people actually be right?

Their interest stirred, Piersom and Claudine began to attend some of the meetings of the so-called Mennists. The teaching that they heard from the Scriptures was rich, filled with many truths they had never been taught before.

Then had come stunning news. Gillis van Aken, a man who had preached and baptized much, had been captured. He had immediately and totally recanted. Rumor even said that he had at one time been guilty of adultery. How disappointed they had been. How could this be the right way?

But conviction from God's Word gripped them. Suppose not all were like him?

At last they decided to attend another meeting. They listened to Leenaert Bouwens explain that one must become a new person in Christ and amend his ways to follow God. This seemed to be the missing ingredient in their own lives and in the state church, which they saw more and more clearly was not following the Scriptures. These people had an entirely different faith and outlook on life. She and Piersom had longed for the settled peace and joy they seemed to have, and hungered for the new life that the Scriptures promised. "Therefore if any man be in Christ, he is a new creature: old things are passed away; behold, all things are become new."[14] Gradually they had come to realize that it was only Christ who could give them the real peace and happiness that they longed for.

Claudine could still recall how they had felt drawn to return many times, and how they had one day knelt in prayer, confessing themselves sinners and in the Name of Jesus asking God to take away their sins and to be the Master of their lives.

She could remember quite clearly the day they had been baptized by Leenaert Bouwens—nearly a year after they were converted. The leaders in Brugge had suggested that Claudine should first learn to read so that she could study the Scriptures for herself. Baptism was not a step to take quickly or lightly. It could mean the ultimate baptism by blood as well. Many a believer had waited a year or even several years until the leaders felt he knew the Scriptures well enough and had proved the genuineness of his faith before he was baptized.

Claudine's reverie was interrupted by a

weary Pieter. "Mother, can you carry me? I'm tired."

"Why, we're almost home. I didn't realize we had come this far already," she commented to Piersom. "Yes, Pieter, I will carry you."

"I thought you were missing the scenery," Peirsom said, smiling. "Maybe after we get these little ones tucked in you can tell me what you were thinking about."

The following is the Dutch version of the hymn sung by the believers in the woods.

Mijn God waer sal ic henen gaen
    Wilt my op uwe wegen stueren
De viant coemt nacht en dach om my staen
    En wil mijn siele verschueren
O Herr laet mi v geest ontfaen
So blijf ick op uwe wegen staen
Dat ick wt'tboeck des leuens niet worde
    gedaen

Doen ick noch in Egypten sadt vast
    Den ruymen ghinc ick treden
Doen was ick ghesien end een weert gast
    Van de werelt was ick doen in vreden
Doen was ick vast in sduyuels strick

"Whom Shall I Fear?"

Mijn leuen was afgryselyck
Den duyuel diende ick seer vlytelyck.

Doen ick my totten Heer begaf
    En my van der werelt ghinck keeren
En liet my helpen wt das boss geslacht
    En versaecte Antechrists leeren
Doen wert ick beghect ende seer versmaet
Omdat ick verachte Babels raet
De gerechtige worden altijt gehaet.

Alsmen oock leest van Abel fijn
    Sacharias wiltet niet vergeten
Daniel worde met valschen schijn
    Inden cuyl der leeuwen gesmeten
So hebben sy de propheten gedaen
En Christus selue wilt dit verstaen
De Apostolen en syn niet vry ghegaen.

Veel lieuer kies ick ongemack
    Al met Gods kinderen te lyden
Dan ick van Pharao ontfang sijn schat
    Om een cleyne tijt met hem te verbliden
Pharaos rijck is titelic
Christus rijck duert eewelyc
Hi ontfangt sijn kinder seer blydelyck.

Chapter 3

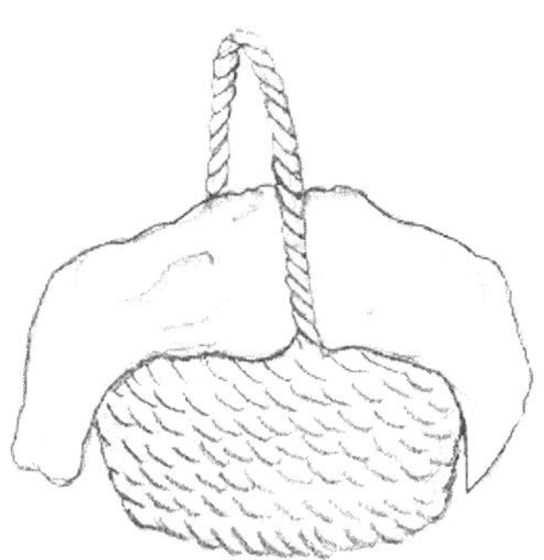

Claudine breathed a sigh of relief. The breakfast dishes had been washed, the beds made, and the house tidied. The children were playing nicely too. So maybe she could start on that pile of mending.

She had just picked up her thread and scissors when a panting, red-faced Piersom burst through the door. "Claudine, we must flee! They're coming to arrest me!"

Claudine stood stunned. Questions flew through her mind in one mad rush. "What should I get? How much time do we have? Where are we going? Where should I begin?"

Margriete, overhearing what was said, ran sobbing to her father. "Father, don't let them take you!"

As Piersom hushed his little daughter, Claudine quickly asked, "What shall I do?"

"Just take enough clothing to keep the children warm if we're outside after dark. I'll get a little food together. They'll check for me at the mill first, so we have a little time—but hurry!"

All this was spoken while Piersom rushed about collecting their Bible, the martyr book, and a book of hymns. These few cherished books must not be left behind to the mercy of calloused people.

"Come along, Margriete." The pale and trembling Margriete followed along behind her mother. Unshed tears shone in her eyes, and she tried in vain to blink them away. Wicked men wanted to come and take her father, her security, away from her. It was almost more than her six years of experience could cope with.

Claudine's own heart was far from calm as she tried to calm her little daughter. "God will take care of us, Margriete. Please bring me the blanket from Nicolas's bed." Keeping Margriete busy would be a help in more ways than one. As Margriete handed her the blanket, Claudine said, "Now put on the boys' shoes for me please. And yours too," she added.

Claudine rushed about with frenzied speed, trying desperately to think of everything they might need. She tossed the things into her big market basket. What if the soldiers arrived before they left? She quickened her step. Her ears were tuned, half expecting at any moment to hear the sound of horses' hooves or rude pounding at the door. More than once, she paused for an instant, thinking she had heard something. Too tense and preoccupied to pray an eloquent prayer, many times in those few minutes she breathed, "Lord, keep us safe."

In a surprisingly short time, though to Claudine it seemed an eternity, everything was collected and ready for the unexpected journey. She and the children joined Piersom in the kitchen, where he had just finished putting some food together in a bundle that would be easy to carry. "Is there room in your basket yet for these books?" he asked. "They must not be seen, you know."

"Yes, I think so."

While Claudine tucked the books deep into their hiding place, Piersom ran to the door and looked up and down the street. He closed the door again. "No one's coming yet. We can't afford to leave without asking God's protection." Taking Margriete's and Pieter's hands in his, he bowed his head, and Claudine bowed her own.

Piersom prayed aloud. "Heavenly Father, You know our needs just now. We ask that You will guide us to safety if it is Your will. Watch over us and our little ones. Help us to be submitted to Your plan for us. In Jesus' Name. Amen."

"Now, we'll go out the back door and take the back streets away from the mill and out of the city. You children walk nicely, and don't talk to anyone we meet. Do you understand?"

They understood.

Piersom picked up Nicolas and the bundle of food and headed out the door. Margriete followed, and Claudine came last, her market basket in one hand and Pieter's hand in the other. Pieter had plied his father with questions while Piersom was packing the food, but now he seemed content to walk along peacefully. Claudine was thankful.

They hurried along as fast as was possible for the children. The clomp of their wooden shoes seemed to echo loudly, announcing their departure to all the world. This was no relaxing stroll. Though outwardly calm, Piersom and Claudine were tense and alert. Were they arousing anyone's suspicions as they quickly walked along? What should they do if they chanced to meet a soldier?

Piersom took the family through back streets and parts of the city that Claudine hardly knew. Brugge was known to be a beautiful city with its many canals and bridges, but today the fleeing family never thought of its beauty as they walked along. At last they neared the city's edge. Knowing they were leaving the city behind gave some relief to their tension. The minutes had seemed like hours as they had traveled, not knowing at what instant their escape might be detected and thwarted.

When they were outside of Brugge, they noticed that up ahead the dirt road entered a wooded area. To the family on the run, it looked sheltering.

"Why don't we leave the road and walk back into those woods far enough to be out of sight and hearing distance? The little ones need a rest, and we could eat some lunch. We can rest too, collect our thoughts, and decide what to do next."

Claudine was pleased with Piersom's suggestion. Although she had relaxed somewhat when they had left the city, it still seemed dangerous to be on the road. She had to constantly resist the urge to glance over her shoulder to make sure there were no soldiers coming to apprehend them. She was surely ready to sit down and rest.

It took them some time to pick their way through the trailless woods to a spot that seemed secluded and safe. Claudine unpacked some food for their lunch. The children seemed content to sit quietly and rest. As they bowed their heads to thank God for the food, they thanked Him too for bringing them safely out of the city.

After Piersom's prayer, Claudine handed bread and cheese to each of the children and to him. Everyone was hungry after their long morning walk.

"Piersom, how did you find out that they were coming to arrest you?"

"Neighbor Hans, the one who lives beside the mill, gave me warning. He's on the council, you know. He's just like a lot of others; he doesn't really support the Inquisition, but he's afraid to say too much. Anyway, when he heard they were coming for me, he hurried right to the mill and warned me to get out of the city."

"That was kind of him. But now what are we going to do? Do you have any idea where you want to go?" Now that they seemed safe enough for the present, Claudine's thoughts turned to this undiscussed subject.

"I don't know for sure, but I've been thinking. The road we're on leads south to Meenen. There are a number of brethren there. Perhaps they could help us find a place to live and get us established among them. It seems to me that might be best. What do you think?"

"I'm sure you know better than I. It sounds like a good idea. But how long will it take us to get there?" Claudine wondered.

"With the children, who can't travel very fast, I think it will take at least two days. I'm almost certain that we cannot reach Meenen by tomorrow evening."

Piersom paused to think, a troubled expression clouding his face. "Where will we sleep? With so many people fleeing to other cities to escape persecution, people are becoming more suspicious of travelers. I'm not sure it's safe to ask strangers for a place to sleep. And these autumn nights can get cool. Do you think we could keep the children warm if we were to sleep under the stars?"

Claudine thought a bit. "It would depend on how cool it gets. Maybe we should wait until this evening to decide. There's not much we can do about it now anyway, is there? We'll just have to pray and trust the Lord to supply our needs."

"You are right." A smile replaced the lines of care on Piersom's face. "Thanks for the encouragement. Are we ready to start walking again?" He stooped to pick up Nicolas, who had fallen asleep.

As the day wore on, the children seemed to be reaching the limit of their endurance. Piersom and Claudine themselves could hardly go on much longer. Carrying a sleeping toddler and their bundles was no easy task.

Pieter, who was almost four, was too small to realize that his father had all he could manage. "Father, I'm tired. Can you carry me?" Poor Pieter was nearly in tears. Already they had slowed their pace and rested often for this tired little fellow. His complaints were coming more often. "Why don't we go home?"

"Pieter, we can't! Bad men would find Father and take him to prison." This emphatic response came from Margriete. "I'm tired too, and my feet hurt so bad, but we can't go home."

Claudine pitied her poor children. At least Margriete was being brave about it. "Piersom, what shall we do?" she wondered.

Piersom surveyed their surroundings. "Why don't we stop and sit down in that grassy spot up ahead? Although it's early, we could eat a little supper. Maybe that would help the children feel better. I'm sure you could use a rest too."

They settled down along the roadside to rest their weary, aching bodies. Pieter stretched out and fell asleep.

This was an unsettling experience for them all. Piersom and Claudine both knew that they would likely never find it safe to return to Brugge. So quickly their lives had changed completely. Claudine had been thinking as they walked along of all the friends they had left without saying good-bye. Would they know what had become of them? She thought with regret of all the household belongings she had left behind. The beds, the spinning wheel, the dishes and kettles, the soap and candles she had worked so hard to make—everything.

How could she ever manage with only the meager things they had with them? Piersom had a few coins in his pocket, but that would not reach very far. Many of the things she had left behind were special to her. There were quilts and dishes from her mother and grandmother that she could hardly bear to part with. She had been feeling so poor and needy as they walked along, stripped of all but the few things they carried with them. And yet, she reminded herself, she was rich. Their family circle was still complete. She would gladly give up all her possessions to keep their family together. What would she do without Piersom?

Piersom too had been thinking. He was leaving a congregation behind. Was he shirking his responsibility? He hated to desert his place as a leader, but there were other leaders there to continue the work. Also he was feeling troubled about the needs of his family. Just how would he manage to provide for his family? He had left behind home, belongings, occupation—everything.

And were they safe yet? The responsibility for his family's safety weighed heavily upon his mind. Suppose the Inquisitors traced them to Meenen. Maybe they even now were on their trail. It was not pleasant to feel like a hunted animal.

But as the family along the roadside paused to thank God for their food and once again commit their troubles to Him, both Piersom and Claudine felt refreshed and encouraged to keep on trusting God to meet their needs. He had protected them this far, and they could trust Him with their futures.

Suddenly Margriete pointed down the road. "Someone's coming!"

All eyes turned toward the man who was walking toward them.

Once again Piersom and Claudine felt that knot of tension that always surfaced when they met people. The stranger was rapidly drawing nearer. The family attempted to continue eating as though nothing was unusual with their being there.

The stranger seemed to be observing them and was slowing his steps. Claudine thought he looked like a harmless old gentleman, but she hoped he would pass on and not bother them.

However, the elderly man was not so inclined. He paused by the roadside and said, "Good day!" His eyes took in the little group, and he smiled as his gaze rested on the snoring Pieter.

"Good day, sir," Piersom said politely.

"Nice warm day, isn't it?" the stranger continued.

"Yes, it is," Piersom responded cautiously.

"Are you traveling far?"

Piersom hesitated, not sure to what extent he could trust this stranger. "Yes, we have quite a distance to travel."

Claudine noticed that Piersom did not say where they were going.

"Well, I know I'm taking a chance when I ask this, but . . ." The elderly stranger paused. "Are you people perhaps fleeing to another city for safety?"

Piersom's uncertainty about how to answer the question made the answer quite obvious.

"Don't be afraid of me. I'm harmless. So many people are having to do that these days, and when I saw your little family here, I just thought that might be the case with you. My own son had to take his family and flee for his life." The man's eyes filled with tears as he spoke of his son.

"These are terrible times," he continued as he shook his head sadly. "Now tell me, do you have a place to spend the night? We live in the next village, and my wife would gladly give you a warm meal and a bed for the night."

Piersom and Claudine looked at each other, silently weighing their decision. What was this man saying? Did he not know that to harbor an Anabaptist* could cost him his life? It had happened before that some had been sentenced to death for giving lodging to the believers. Was this a trap?

But the man seemed sincere, and the way he had spoken of his son helped to allay their fears. Piersom said, "Thank you for your kindness. It would be nice for the children to have a place for the night."

"Very well. I will go on and tell my wife. You come at your own pace. There's no need for us to introduce ourselves; it will be safer that way." After carefully explaining the way to his home, the man continued down the road.

Piersom and Claudine soon gathered their things and started on again. Piersom was grateful that God had been so good to them in providing a place for the night. Claudine felt a bit fearful for their safety though. "Suppose he went on ahead to report us to the authorities," she said to Piersom.

"I don't think he will, and we must trust God. Somehow I trust him. Maybe it's the way

*Name given to the Mennists because they practiced believer's baptism and were baptized again, not considering infant baptism valid.

he spoke of his son. It would have been dangerous for him to be seen leading us to his house," Piersom said.

Yes, that was true. Claudine had not thought of that.

Knowing there was rest ahead seemed to give the family new strength to continue on, and soon they reached the village and found the man's home, just as he had directed. His wife welcomed them warmly.

After enjoying a warm meal, Claudine took the weary children straight to bed. But Piersom wanted to visit more with his host.

"Are you a believer?" he asked the man.

"Well, there are so many different beliefs." The old man hedged. "How would you know who's right? There are the Calvinists, the Lutherans, and the Anabaptists. Of all the groups, I think the Anabaptists are the most correct. If I don't miss my guess, that's where you belong?"

"We prefer to simply call ourselves brethren; or some call us Mennists, after one of our former leaders, Menno Simons. Yes, that's where we fit in," Piersom acknowledged.

"I thought so. I haven't gone so far as to join any group. I know there are things in the

Catholic Church presently that aren't right, but I still go to Mass." His voice trailed off into empty silence. After a moment he continued. "Although you people live it about the best, if I would join, I'd just be asking for trouble. But as I was saying, I'm not impressed with some of these groups who broke off from the state church. They're no better. If they could get enough people on their side, they would make theirs the state church, and persecute anyone who does not comply."

Piersom nodded. "That's where we differ with them. A church must be separate from the state in order to be a pure church. That's the very basis of our separating from the state church. The Bible teaches that we must be separated from anything evil and the church must consist of people who are all righteous and have chosen to follow God. When babies are baptized into the church and everyone else is a member because they are required to be, there is sure to be wickedness in the church. I can't be a part of a church like that."

"And these other groups think they can fight to protect themselves, and make as much trouble as they want. I've even heard of Lutherans who hold a Bible in one hand and a glass of beer in the other. Then they think they're so right." The man spoke vehemently.

"Such things are not right, even as many things in the Catholic Church are not right, and to live true to the Scriptures we've had to come out from it and be separate," Piersom said. He had been listening quietly to his talkative host, but now he had something he wanted to say. "All of us, those people included, will one day give an account of our lives before God. But what about you? You know what's right, and you'll have to answer before God for what you did with the truth too. Don't be afraid to be counted among the righteous, even if it means personal danger. If you're ashamed of Christ now, He will not claim you either in the world to come. Life is serious. Are you where God wants you to be?"

The old man listened agreeably, but he still did not want to make any decision that would change his life. Piersom was burdened for this man who, like so many others, knew the truth and appreciated those who followed it, but did not want to pay the high price of living that way himself.

The next morning the man who had graciously given them lodging insisted upon taking them in his wagon to the outskirts of Meenen. Claudine silently thanked God for so wonderfully meeting the needs of their children on this unexpected journey.

Chapter 4

It was nearing bedtime one summer evening when Piersom and Claudine had just finished reading from the Scriptures and praying with their children. Such a joy it was to be able to enjoy normal family routines again. The children had gone to play, and Piersom and Claudine sat talking.

They had been in Meenen for nearly a year. It was now the summer of 1566. Pauwels van Meenen, Jacques the candlemaker, and Piersom all filled their places in leading the group of believers that met in fields and other secluded spots around Meenen and Kortrijk.

"As you know, I met today with Jacques and Pauwels," Piersom began. "I am fearful that more troubles are ahead for all of us with this spreading iconoclasm." Piersom talked in low tones so that the children would not notice what he was saying. "The brethren said that there was quite a riot in Brugge. The Calvinists and the Lutherans want to force their own way, however they can. They marched through the streets to the Catholic Church and completely wrecked it. The windows are broken and the altars smashed; the place is in shambles—or so it is reported in the village. It's been happening in other cities too. They smash statues, burn church furniture, chase the monks from the monasteries, and wreck the monasteries as well."

Claudine was not unaware of these latest happenings. "How can they think theirs is the right way? Nowhere does the Bible teach us to act like that. They're making it harder for themselves. I'm sure the authorities will feel even less inclined to be lenient with them now."

Piersom agreed. "And they make it more difficult for us too. But the only thing we can do is to absolutely refuse to have anything to do with these revolts. You know, people are trying to figure out why we don't get involved. A lot of the Inquisitors and authorities don't want people to know that we believe it's wrong to resist evil against us. They are putting up posters and sending out writings telling people that we are just being clever and trying to get a large following before we start our resistance. They want people to think that that is our reason for rejecting this violence."

"But that's not correct. How can we show people that we have deeper reasons than that?"

"I guess we really can't, Claudine. At least they do know that we won't help with this destruction. We'll just have to go on living the way God would have us to, and let them think what they will."

"Do you think this will bring more persecution?" Claudine asked anxiously, concern clouding her face.

"I'm almost certain it will."

Claudine's spirits drooped under the weight of this new worry. "You know, Piersom, I just can't help wishing sometimes that Regent Margaret would have listened to those councilmen who went to her this spring and asked her to stop the Inquisition. Think how that would be. So far we've lived here, enjoying normal family life, and it's so nice. But there's always the uncertainty of the future hanging over us. If the Inquisition would have been stopped, we could enjoy life and serve God with never a fear that we might suffer for it. Can you imagine how that would be? It seems that it would be so wonderful. But now with this new trouble, I have a feeling that darker days are ahead for all of us."

Piersom sensed the struggles engaging his wife's heart and tried to find words to encourage her. "You can be sure that God is able to give courage and strength if we are called to face suffering. He has helped others to come through, and you know how we are inspired by their strength and courage."

Yes, they had witnessed the sufferings of some of their own brethren. Claudine had always marveled at their calmness and courage and their testimonies of how God was with them. But still, she shuddered to think of the possibility of facing it herself.

Piersom went on. "Sometimes I think that if we had no suffering, we would perhaps enjoy this life too much and not look forward to heaven. We might start thinking that we have control of our lives, and lose our faith in God. The Bible promises persecution, you know. I'd rather suffer than lose out because life is too comfortable. God will still watch over us, even in hard times. If He sees the sparrow fall, can you not realize how much more He cares about us and our hurts?"[15]

"I know you're right, but sometimes I forget and need to be reminded. What would I do without you to listen to my struggles?" She squeezed his hand as she rose to her feet. "I think it's time for me to get our little ones to bed. Come, children. Let's get washed for bed." Hearing their mother's call, the children came obediently.

Piersom watched thoughtfully as his wife and children put away the few simple playthings and prepared for the night. Sudden appreciation welled up within him for this little family circle with which God had blessed him. His gaze rested on his wife. She was undoubtedly a beautiful woman, not only of face but also in character. The neat veiling covering most of her blond hair was a true symbol of her submission to him as her husband. He deeply appreciated her many good qualities: her faith, her honesty, her motherly guidance of the children, her openness and submission to him, her cheerful spirit that often bubbled forth in song. He wondered what he would do without her. She held the household together and kept things running smoothly in such a wonderful way. He told himself that he must once again thank her for being such a good wife and mother.

Chapter 5

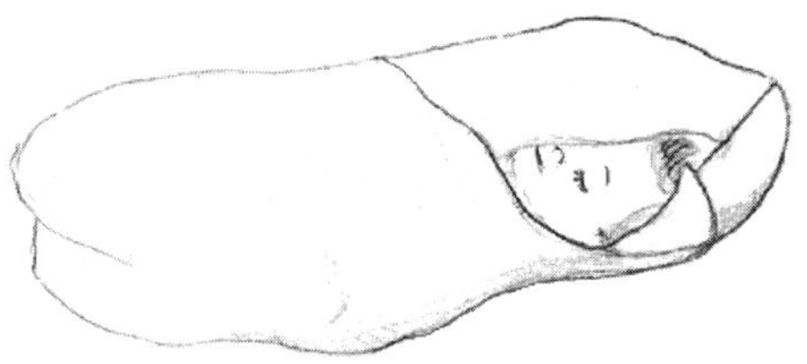

Claudine carefully dropped the tiny seeds into the row she had made with a pointed stick. It was a warm spring day, perfect for planting garden. The children, invigorated with the warm sunshine, raced about, shouting and laughing.

Claudine was counting her blessings as she worked. The Lord had been so good to them. The beautiful outdoors made it easy to think on the bright side of things. They had passed two winters here at Meenen, and thus far had been undisturbed. She was so thankful for this blessing, though she never knew how long it would last, for others around them had not been so blessed.

As she worked, her thoughts turned to another blessing to be counted. Before many days passed, another child would be born into their home. It seemed she had planned and dreamed about this child's coming for so long. Would it be a sister for Margriete, or another son? She would be happy for either, so long as it was healthy and normal, God willing. A stab of worry threatened to dampen her spirits again. But, no, she must trust the Lord. He who created her and her little one could bring that little one safely into the world. She would not let fears of complications trouble her.

With the expectation of the birth of this child came also the concern for keeping its coming a secret. The Catholic priest must not hear news of a new baby. It could mean trouble for them if he did, as they did not intend to have it baptized. Claudine was grateful that she had a trustworthy friend, Deacon Jacques's wife, to be with her for the birth.

She wondered what the future held in store for this little one she already loved and was so eager to meet. The dangers were greater now than ever. Ever since the iconoclasm had spread across the country, the authorities had been busier than ever, hunting out all those who were disloyal to the Catholic Church.

Piersom and Claudine often prayed for their unborn child as well as for the rest of their children. Claudine could not help but hope and pray that God would protect their little ones from suffering. She had seen the grief that children went through when their parents were taken. She simply could not allow herself to dwell on the thought of how her own children might respond should this happen to her or Piersom. As she considered all these uncertainties, she could only take her burdens to God and entrust the future of her family into His care. Overpowering all her doubts and fears was the knowledge of God's promise that He would always be faithful in meeting their needs, though it might not be just the way she would have chosen.

One morning soon after the sun had risen, a tired but exuberant Claudine cradled her newborn son, Jan, in her arms. She gazed long into his tiny face. The ruddy, wrinkled countenance was beautiful to her. Piersom too was overjoyed as they together inspected their fragile little bundle. Another blessing from God to enjoy, but an added responsibility—a soul that would never die, entrusted to them to mold and shape as they chose. "What an awesome responsibility for unworthy human hands!" Claudine thought to herself.

Claudine smiled at the welcome the tiny blanketed bundle received from his sister and brothers. The children dearly loved their new brother and never seemed to tire of holding him. She was very grateful for Deacon Jacques's wife's faithful help. When Claudine felt strong enough, the deacon's wife went back to her own responsibilities.

Parents and children alike enjoyed Jan's first smiles, watched anxiously when he seemed sick, hurried to calm him when he cried, and cheered him on when he learned something new.

Often Claudine sat musing as she gazed into the round face of her small son. What did the future hold for him? Would he grow up to be a faithful servant of God? Did she and Piersom really know how to train children in the right way? She often marveled that children are so teachable, so quick to believe whatever they are told. But it seemed such a weighty task to instill in them all that they needed to know to become useful, God-fearing adults. And, oh, the terrible results if they should fail! When she thought of that possibility, a plea for wisdom often ascended from the mother heart on the rocker.

At times as she studied her innocent, sleeping baby, she wondered, "Will I live to see him grow up? Or will the Lord return and take us all home to heaven while our children are all in safe innocence? What a wonderful, peaceful way to go," she often mused. "No grief, no suffering, no pain, no loved ones left behind. Lord, help me that, regardless of what the future holds for me, I will be able to carry out my responsibilities faithfully, and one day meet You without regret."

Chapter 6

An unusually humid summer day was drawing to a close, and Claudine felt weary and spent. She hurried with the dishes, eager to be finished so that she could sit down to rest. A smile crossed her face as she glanced at Piersom. He was relaxing in a chair nearby after a hard day's work, enjoying his children. Jan was sleeping on one arm, while the other arm encircled Nicolas, who was sitting on his knee. Margriete and Pieter were interrupting each other, chattering to their father about the little things that were so important in their childish world.

Knock! Knock! Knock!

Piersom partly rose to his feet and stood Nicolas down, intending to go to the door, but the door burst open. A man whom Claudine recognized as one on the town council stepped inside.

"Piersom, run for your life. Titelman is on his way to get you." With that he turned and was gone, not wanting to be found when the Inquisitors arrived.

Again the scene of peaceful family life was changed to confusion and terror. Claudine stepped forward and took the baby while Piersom tried to free himself from the crying children.

Claudine spoke urgently above the noise. "Piersom, go quickly out back to the woods!"

"But you must come too! I can't leave you here!" Piersom said.

"Oh, please go quickly! I'll join you as soon as I can," Claudine urged.

Piersom swung around and ran out the back door. As Claudine turned to comfort the children, she noticed that neighbors were coming into their yard. The Inquisitors must be near. Then above the growing noise outside, Claudine heard the sound of hoofbeats. The Inquisitors were coming. She must flee. But how could she run with the children? She hesitated an instant, and then with Jan still in her arms, quickly stepped out the back door.

She had just left the house when she heard the front door burst open. The woods looked hopelessly far away. She clutched Jan tightly to her breast and took a few desperate steps in that direction.

Suddenly her heart despaired as she heard a shout, "There goes the wife of the man you want, with a baby in her arms!"

In moments she was seized and found herself confronting the Inquisitor, the dreaded Pieter Titelman.

His first hard words were drowned out by the familiar cry of Margriete, mingled with Pieter's and Nicolas's. Oh, how the cries of her frightened children tore at her heart as they rushed to her and flung their arms about her skirts, sobbing wildly. As she shifted Jan to one arm and tried to comfort them, they were ruthlessly torn from her and set aside. Kind neighbors drew them close and tried in vain to calm them. Claudine cared not what she might face; she could hardly bear to see her children suffer such grief and fear.

A soldier was left to guard her while

Titelman and his other helpers searched the house for Piersom. Claudine took advantage of the few moments and called her children to her. She kissed and hugged them while they clung to her, weeping. She stooped down to whisper words of comfort in their ears. But what could she say when her own heart was threatening to overflow in a flood of tears? She must be calm for their sakes. There would be plenty of time for tears later. What would become of these dear children? Would she ever see them again?

The Inquisitors returned from their fruitless search and stood about, deciding what to do with their captive. Would it work to put her in the prison at Meenen?

"You remember what happened the last time we imprisoned someone in a town that did not have city walls," one of them said. "The people broke open the prison and let four hundred prisoners free. We can't keep her here."

They had kept a wary eye on the crowd as they discussed the problem of where to take their captive. This crowd did not appear to be sympathetic with them. Hisses of "Judas" and "Traitor" could be heard, and angry glares were aimed at the man who had pointed out Claudine.

It was soon decided that they would take her

to Ypres, and one of the bailiffs was sent to bring a wagon. Before long Claudine was roughly commanded to climb aboard, and her trip to prison began.

Pulling Jan close, Claudine bowed her head and gave vent to the tears that had been threatening, the sound of her children's frightened crying echoing in her ears. If only her young, innocent children would not have to suffer through this dreadful nightmare. Almost she wished she had no children.

After the first flood of tears was past, she began to pray. Her head remained bowed over her little one throughout the ten-mile ride to Ypres. Instinctively she turned to her heavenly Father for comfort, as she had learned to do in trying times before. She told herself that the God who controls the whole universe could keep her children in His care. He who sees the sparrow fall would also see and provide for the needs of her three motherless children. And yet, as the sun was setting, she grieved to think of the terrors this night would hold for them as they cried for their mother. So much did she think of her children that she scarcely thought about what might lie in store for her.

She was glad she had not been forced to hand

Jan over to someone else. She marveled that they had not taken him from her. Perhaps they knew he needed his mother's nourishment. Whatever the reason, she thanked God that she was spared that separation.

The town of Ypres was shrouded in darkness as the wagon entered through the city gates and rumbled down the cobblestone street. Just ahead, casting a long shadow over the moonlit street, loomed a dark stone castle, its pointed spires piercing the night sky. Claudine shivered at the sight of it, yet felt a surprising calm within. She knew that God would be with her. She was not going to prison as a criminal, but as a Christian. Surely the Lord would stand by her side.

Chapter 7

Piersom hurried into the woods. He pushed frantically on until he was certain that he was out of sight; then he sat down to wait for Claudine.

He waited tensely, restlessly, a gnawing dread beginning to rise within as the minutes slipped by. "What's keeping her? Why doesn't she come? Why, oh, why didn't I insist that she come with me immediately? Maybe she didn't realize the closeness of the danger and didn't leave in time."

Then a comforting thought came. "Maybe it was just me they wanted and she'll come when she can slip out here unseen, and let me know. Oh, please, Lord, bring her safely here. Forgive me for even leaving her."

Piersom began pacing the forest floor in agitation as the minutes crept by and there still was no sign of Claudine. The longer he waited, the greater his dread became. Oh, how could he bear it if Claudine should be taken?

At last he could stand it no longer. Cautiously, he headed back the way he had come, straining to see through the woods. There was yet a chance that she could be coming. Now he could see their house. Crouching behind the bushes, he peered through the tangled branches.

His hand flew to his mouth to muffle the cry that escaped his lips. There, starting down the road, was a wagon bearing Claudine and Jan. Never had they looked so precious to him as they did then. And so helpless and alone. He resisted the urge to run and try to rescue them. He knew it was impossible. He strained to see. No, none of the other children were along—just Claudine and Jan. The soldiers on horseback accompanying the wagon left no doubt about what was happening.

But where were they going? That was not the way to the Meenen prison. Where were they taking his wife?

He must leave this spot or he would be seen. It was not safe here. With shoulders bowed under an invisible burden, he quickly picked his way deeper into the woods. Finding a secluded spot, he sat down and bowed his head in his hands. Why had he not stayed with Claudine? Why had he not insisted that she flee with him? Over and over he blamed himself as hot tears streamed down his face and dropped onto his beard. Gladly, oh, how gladly, he would exchange places with her. Indeed, it would be much easier to suffer himself than to think of all that she likely would have to face. He shuddered. Not many came out of the prisons alive, unless they escaped—or recanted.

As that thought struck him, he groaned. "O Lord, give her courage. Don't let her give up the faith. And spare her from suffering if it is Your will." He paused in anguish of spirit. "Lord, bring her back to me," he entreated. But even as he prayed, he knew that many others had not been returned to their loved ones. Difficult as it was, he knew he must pray, "Lord, Thy will be done."

Heedless of the passing of time and the fall of night around him, Piersom sat thinking and praying. At last he accepted the fact that God in His sovereignty had allowed things to happen as they had. He would have to trust Him, whatever the future might hold, although he could not understand why God should allow such terrible things to take place. He would commit Claudine to the Lord, who loved her as much as he did. The Lord was capable of meeting her needs, even now when he was helpless to do anything for her.

Then he thought of his children. Margriete, Pieter, Nicolas—where were they? Since darkness had fallen over the land, perhaps it would be safe to venture out. He needed to talk to someone and find out where they were taking Claudine. And he must try to find the children. He could imagine how distressed they must be.

The stars were shining brightly when Piersom cautiously left the shelter of the woods. He hoped that because of the hour, the streets would be deserted. Still he took a roundabout way and avoided going near his home. He had decided to go to the home of the man who had warned him.

Quickly and quietly he glided through a maze of deserted back streets. Soon he was knocking at the back door of his friend's home.

All was dark, but in a few moments he heard someone stirring within. The door opened. Recognizing Piersom, the councilman grabbed his shoulder and pulled him inside, bolting the door behind him. He groped about the room, making certain all the windows were covered before lighting a lamp. This done, he returned and invited Piersom to be seated with him at the table.

With halting words and shaking voice, the councilman spoke first. "Piersom, I'm sorry. I guess by now you know they took your wife."

Piersom tried to answer around the lump in his throat. He had thought his emotions were under control, but to talk about it was a difficult thing. "Yes, I was out in the woods waiting for her to come. She told me to go and she would come soon. But when she didn't come, my fears mounted, and I crept back to the edge of the woods and saw them leaving with her." He stopped, unable to go on.

The councilman cleared his throat gruffly, uncertain what to say. "I wish I had come sooner," he said.

"Where did they take her?" Piersom asked quietly.

"To Ypres. It sounded as though they did

not trust keeping her here, because there's no city wall, and if she would escape from prison, she would be hard to find. Also, I don't think they trusted the crowd that had gathered in your yard. The people were upset with that neighbor man of yours. I'm disgusted at him too! Your wife had started for the woods when your neighbor across the street pointed her out to the bailiff. If he hadn't betrayed her, she would likely be with you now.

"The crowd was angry, calling him 'Judas' and 'traitor.' As soon as they left with your wife, the crowd chased him out of town, and he'll not be welcome here again! Serves him right!" He slammed his fist on the table to emphasize his disgust.

Piersom slowly shook his head. "They shouldn't have done that. He probably is sorry now that he betrayed her, and besides that, he's driven from his home. The Lord says, 'Vengeance is mine; I will repay.'[16] It would have been better to leave things in God's hands."

The councilman sat gazing at Piersom, plainly astonished. "How can you say that? Didn't you understand me right? He's the man responsible for your wife being in prison."

"I understand. But, my friend, God's Word

tells me to love my enemies."

The councilman shook his head again. "I don't understand you people. I couldn't accept it so easily if it were my wife."

"I love my wife very dearly, and I can't begin to tell you how much it grieves me to have her suffer." The anguish on his face confirmed the truth of his words. "But by God's grace, I will love my enemies and forgive them, and do good to them if I have the chance."

"And then they persecute you people! It's not fair."

"All will be fair on the Judgment Day."

"I know," the councilman agreed.

"Where are my children?" Piersom wondered.

"The young couple who live next door to you took them in. I'm sure they're taking good care of them."

"Do you think it would be safe for me to go there now to see the children? I expect they're quite upset."

"Probably you'd be safe at this hour," the councilman answered.

Piersom rose to his feet, thanked his friend for his bold effort, and bade him a sober good-bye. Then he disappeared into the dark night.

The councilman had promised to keep his household possessions for him, so he would not go to his home. First, he must see the children, and he had determined what he would do then. Under the cover of darkness, he would start for Ypres. There would be no sleep anyway, and he could think and pray just as well while he walked.

Chapter 8

Jan was crying. Claudine sat up, blinking and bewildered. Where was she? Why did she feel so stiff and cramped? As the memory of the past evening hit her, her spirits drooped. She was in prison! Quickly she grabbed the crying, squirming Jan and began to feed him. She could tell by the faint light that it must be early morning.

Now that she had Jan quieted, she had plenty of time to think. All sleepiness was gone. Her time of testing had come. She felt a surge of panic. Was she ready to handle this? Her mind seemed to search for some way to escape this horrible plight and get back to the normal life she had been enjoying yesterday. Was it really just yesterday that she had been free? It seemed so long ago.

As she had done so often before, the instinct rose within to pour out her troubles to Piersom. He had always been there when she needed him, and now—he was not here! Only now did she realize just how much she had always depended on him. She felt so alone and unable to face the dark future that rose like a formidable mountain before her.

The thought of Piersom and the children brought a fresh burst of tears. Would she ever stop crying? She had cried long into the night before she had fallen asleep, and now here she was, crying again. She must come to grips with this before her fellow prisoners woke up and found her weeping again.

She had only one place to turn for help. She bowed her head and pleaded silently to God for strength, for calmness, for courage. The Lord was able to help her, even more than Piersom could have. She prayed for wisdom to answer her accusers. As she prayed for Piersom and for Margriete, Pieter, and Nicolas, the tears flowed unchecked. Had Piersom escaped? How were the children getting along? What grief were they suffering? Had they cried themselves to sleep last night? Where were they? Had Piersom returned to them?

She felt so helplessly trapped. Here she was, unable to go to her children, who needed her so much. How could they manage without her? Of course someone would see that they were clothed and fed, but who could soothe their bleeding hearts? Who would teach them about their heavenly Father? She had been awed at times by the way their children had trusted her and Piersom so completely, and now their security had been shattered. Now they were grieving, and she was helpless to do anything about it. Piersom too was grieving, she knew, but at least he was old enough to take care of himself.

But, no, she was not helpless. She could pray, and she found relief in asking God to meet the needs of her children. After all, they were God's children, given to her to care for. Now God had allowed her to be taken away, and He would still care for His own. God was not too small to be entrusted with her precious children. Indeed, they seemed more precious now than ever.

She had found fresh courage in prayer. Now she determined to try to think of promises from the Scriptures to give her strength. She would need something to cling to. In her heart she knew that a difficult road lay ahead for her. She was glad now that she had always found it easy to memorize. Without a Bible, she would need those promises she had tucked away in her memory. The first one that came to her mind was a psalm that she liked to sing. She hummed it quietly to herself. "The Lord is my light and my salvation; whom shall I fear? the Lord is the strength of my life; of whom shall I be afraid?"[17] What a promise! Her fears vanished for the present as she meditated on this promise that had suddenly become very precious.

She glanced down at Jan. He was sound asleep again, secure in Mother's arms. "Little fellow, you haven't a care in the world. You've no idea where you are, nor do you care, so long as you have your mother," she thought. As she squeezed him to herself, that stab of pain returned. She had broken that trust, that security that her three other children also had in her. But, no, it was not her fault. She must not blame herself.

The memory of a recent happening brought sudden tears once more to her burning, swollen eyes. One day not long ago, Nicolas had fallen and cut his knee. He had come to her, expecting her to make it better, and was puzzled that she could not. As she thought of this, she was struck with the idea that she was a child of the God who knew no human limitations. He would not disappoint her trust. She would trust her uncertain future to Him, and that of her children as well.

Taking her eyes off her sleeping son, she looked about her. It had been too dark to see much when she had been thrust into this cell last night. But now the early morning sunlight was beginning to brighten the room from the window high up in the wall. It appeared to her that she must be in a deep underground cell. The thick stone walls allowed very little sunlight to brighten the damp room. She studied the barred window high above her, wondering if there would be any way to escape. No, it seemed impossible with the window so high and with bars to make it secure.

Taking her eyes off the window, she gazed once more about her. The hard earthen floor felt damp and clammy. The room was long and spacious, offering plenty of room for the prisoners to move about. A water bucket stood in one corner. She wondered vaguely how much of her future she would spend in this drab, dreary place. But at least she was not alone.

She turned her attention to her fellow prisoners. Now that she could see better, she was surprised at how many prisoners were in this cell. There were more than she had thought last night. She counted eight men and five women besides herself and Jan. A few looked old and some middle-aged; several looked too young to be here in prison. Claudine's heart went out to them in silent sympathy. Would they be faithful?

She pushed aside a feeling of repulsion at the rumpled, disheveled appearance of her fellow prisoners and at the smell of unclean bodies. They could not help it, and she supposed she soon would look and smell as they did. It was not a pleasant thought. Would she, who had always tried to be neat and clean, soon be like these others?

Most were awake by this time and were stretching and walking about to exercise their cramped muscles. A young woman sat down by Claudine and introduced herself.

"My name is Mayken. Your little boy makes me think of my two children, who were taken from me when I was brought here." She spoke with pensive sadness. "That's the most difficult trial I face. My husband was burned for his faith two years ago."

Claudine understood her grief. "I have three other children besides Jan, and I don't know what will become of them. I was just sitting here thinking of them, and telling myself that they're God's children and that He is able to provide for them. But this awful world holds so many dangers for them." Discouragement was threatening again.

"That's the thing that troubles me." Common suffering bonded the hearts of the two new friends together.

"How long have you been here?" Claudine wondered.

"It's hard to keep track of time, but I think it's been about two months. I've been questioned twice, but I have not yet suffered torture. It's so hard when they just let you sit day after day, but I think they know that too. I pray so much that God will help me to be faithful to Him."

" 'Greater is he that is in you, than he that is in the world.'[18] We must remember that." Claudine was reminding herself as much as Mayken.

"Yes, it's a great help to remember God's

promises," Mayken replied.

As they sat together in companionable silence, Claudine noticed two men who were still lying down in one corner of the cell. She could tell by their moaning now and again when they shifted positions that something was wrong. "What's wrong with them?" she quietly asked.

"They were stretched on the rack. They've been here for six months already, and they've endured much agony the last weeks, with questionings and torture. It's hard to see them suffer so."

Claudine shuddered as she observed their misery. Could she handle such pressure?

One elderly man stepped over and greeted Claudine. "You must be the one who arrived last night. Were you apprehended for your faith too?"

"Yes, I was."

"Be faithful, sister. The crown awaits us. What is your name?"

Claudine told him her name, her husband's name, and the name of the town where they had lived. She learned that his name was Hendrick. He spoke encouragingly to her for a few minutes, and in that short time Claudine could tell that this man's faith and courage would be a real comfort to her. He seemed so selfless, radiating cheer and joy.

As he walked away to join the group of men at the other side of the room, Mayken said in an undertone, "He's so unselfish and wants to encourage everyone else to be faithful. I don't know what we would do without him. He's such an inspiration to us all. He's the oldest one here, and he's like a leader to us."

And just then Hendrick showed that she was right. "Come, everyone. Let's gather together for our morning worship. This time why don't we think of verses to share from memory with each other. We can't let ourselves forget God's Word. Now that we don't have it in our hands, we must keep it in our hearts."

The sharing of verses inspired Claudine more than she could have thought possible. Could it really be that here in prison she could feel such joy in knowing God's love? As she listened thoughtfully to the promises shared by the others, she thought of one portion from the Scriptures that expressed her thoughts:

> Who shall separate us from the love of Christ? shall tribulation, or distress, or persecution, or

famine, or nakedness, or peril, or sword? As it is written, For thy sake we are killed all the day long; we are accounted as sheep for the slaughter. Nay, in all these things we are more than conquerors through him that loved us. For I am persuaded, that neither death, nor life, nor angels, nor principalities, nor powers, nor things present, nor things to come, nor height, nor depth, nor any other creature, shall be able to separate us from the love of God, which is in Christ Jesus our Lord.[19]

Chapter 9

With a jangle of keys, the jailer unlocked the heavy iron door and swung it open. The short, stocky man puffed his way into the cell and plopped a kettle of thin soup onto the floor. Their supper had arrived. Supper usually consisted of a bowl of watery soup and a bit of bread for each. It was meager fare for hungry stomachs.

Claudine was especially glad to see a meal arrive. Her ration of food had to nourish both her and Jan, and it was barely enough. She often experienced the nauseated pangs of an empty stomach. Already she was growing thinner.

As the jailer finished handing out the portions of food, he turned to Claudine. "I was told to inform you that you will appear before the priests tomorrow for questioning."

Claudine nodded wordlessly. She had been wondering when her time would come. Now on the morrow she would face her accusers and speak for herself.

She spent a long time in prayer before falling asleep that night. She prayed that God would guard her lips from revealing anything that would threaten the life of another believer. She asked for a clear mind so that these deceiving people might not be able to confuse her. Jesus promised in the Scriptures that the Holy Spirit would give her the words to say, and she clung to that promise.[20]

Although she did not know whom she would face, she prayed for them, asking God to soften their hearts to accept the truth. And she could not conclude without a prayer of thanks for her fellow prisoners, who no doubt would be praying while she was being questioned.

The next day found Claudine seated before three priests. A clerk joined them to record all that was said. Claudine quickly surveyed each of her accusers. As she scanned their faces, her spirits almost drooped. They looked so sure of themselves as they fixed their condescending gazes upon her. Was there not even one soft heart among them?

The first man to speak had gray hair and appeared to be the oldest. He fixed his gaze sternly upon her. "Have you been rebaptized?"

"I have been baptized with the one true baptism upon the confession of my faith."

"Are you saying then that infant baptism is not a true baptism?"

"I am."

"You are mistaken. The holy baptism of infants is right, according to the Scriptures."

"Where do the Scriptures teach infant baptism?" Claudine asked politely.

"In more than one place you find it. Foolish woman, don't you know anything about the Bible? In the sixteenth chapter of the first epistle to the Corinthians, it says that the whole household of Stephanas were the first in Achaia who addicted themselves to the ministry of the saints. And the jailer with all his household was baptized. And the household of Lydia was baptized as well. Now you see? Would you be so bold as to say that there were no infants in those households?"

"But an infant cannot addict himself to the ministry of the saints, as the Scriptures say of Stephanas's house. And concerning the Philippian jailer, it says that he rejoiced with all his house that he had believed in Christ Jesus. Can an infant rejoice in the faith?" Claudine's question was simply and courteously asked.

The priests were plainly disturbed. After a bit of muttering, one of them quickly spoke up. "So your children aren't baptized then?"

"No."

"I guess they haven't any names either, then."

The priests burst into loud guffaws at this joke. "They have to be given their names when they're baptized," he went on to prove his point.

Claudine said not a word. She must keep her tongue in the spirit of meekness.

Having no more to say on this subject, they quickly seized another. "When have you last been to the Sacrament?"

"I don't remember when it was. Perhaps ten years ago."

"Tell us what you think of it. Why have you not taken part of the body of Christ?"

"I do not believe that it is the body of Christ.

The Scriptures say that Jesus broke bread and gave His disciples bread. He didn't give them pieces of His flesh. He said, 'This do in remembrance of me.'[21] The bread was only a symbol of His body that was broken in crucifixion to redeem sinful mankind." Claudine spoke with a voice clear and firm.

"Oh, bah, silly woman, you don't know anything. Why would a simple woman like you try to teach us what the Scriptures say? It says right there, 'This is my body,' " shouted the gray-haired priest.

Claudine's voice was surprisingly calm in comparison. "But was it His body? The Scriptures say it was broken bread."

One priest who had thus far said little spoke up. "But it became His flesh and made them holy." Without a pause he picked up another subject. "What do you believe concerning the saints? Do you faithfully pray to them?" Propping his hand on his chin, he eyed her sharply.

"The Scriptures tell me that Christ is my only Mediator."[22]

"That's heresy, and if you don't turn from your stubborn ways, you'll have to suffer an intolerable death."

"If God allows it, I am willing to suffer." Claudine again responded calmly.

"Do you mean to say that you have no fear of death? You've never tasted death, you know."

Claudine was amazed at the way the Lord brought answers to her mind. And yet, had He not promised He would? "Christ says, 'If a man keep my saying, he shall never see death.'[23] The rich man who had no pity for Lazarus tasted death, and he'll taste it forever."[24]

The oldest priest spoke up again. His tone was surprisingly soft and pleading. "Wouldn't you like to go to your husband and children again? Think how they must be missing you. How will they ever get along without you? It's hard telling what evil might befall your children if you neglect them so." He suddenly stood to his feet and held a crucifix before her face. "Just kiss this, your lord and god, and you can be free to go. That's simple enough."

Claudine turned her head away and pushed the crucifix from her. "That is not my Lord and God. That's nothing but a wooden idol. Take it away."

"How you do blaspheme! Don't you fear the judgment of God?" He shook his head. "One more question yet. Who baptized you?"

"That I do not wish to tell." Claudine's answer was firm.

"We have ways that might induce you to tell" came the menacing threat.

"The Lord will guard the door of my lips, for you would only use it to the hurt of more innocent people."

"How impudent and foolish you are! We'll send you back to your cell to think on this awhile. Maybe if you sit in prison longer, you'll decide to embrace the true faith so you can be free again. We do have ways of helping people change their minds, you know. The next time you could face the rack or other inducements"—the priest paused with a significant nod—"if you don't give up this foolish stubbornness."

Claudine decided to be brave and make a request. "Could I ask that some food be sent for my baby at mealtime? He is not capable of wrong, even if you think I am, and he's crying with hunger."

The man with the brown beard replied, "Lady, that's your problem. You know how you could solve it." With that, she was dismissed to be returned to her cell and to her son, whom she had left in Mayken's care.

Claudine's heart was heavy. Everything

seemed hopeless. She had thought that if she spoke the truth straight from the Scriptures, they surely could not argue with it. But these men seemed set in their traditions, and nothing had changed their minds. It was frustrating to Claudine. There was nothing to do but pray, for God alone could touch their hearts of stone. Sad it would be on the Judgment Day when they would stand before God with so much innocent blood on their hands. As she thought of that, she determined that even if they would choose to burn her at the stake, it would be better to burn a few moments than to burn forever in the awful fire of hell.

Chapter 10

Day followed day and passed by in monotonous succession. Days turned into weeks and weeks into months. Some days were bright and Claudine was filled with courage, and other days were dark.

At times she could hardly bear the load of grief in her heart. Oh, to be able to lean on Piersom's shoulder and let him share her burdens. How she missed him. In her mind she often pictured him—tall, broad-shouldered, dark-haired Piersom. She tried to picture his brown eyes, those eyes that had so often spoken meaningful messages to her. Where was he?

How was he faring? How was he coping with his load of grief? It must be difficult for him to be thinking of her here in prison. Many prayers ascended from the damp underground cell on his behalf.

And the children—how she longed to see them again, to clasp each of them in her arms and put their troubled minds to rest. In battles of loneliness she could envision a wonderful reunion with Piersom and the children. Lost in her imagination, she could almost forget where she was. It would be like heaven on earth! But, oh, it was too cruel. Such thoughts only made the tears flow once again at the impossibility of carrying out her dreams. Resolutely she tried to push those thoughts from her mind. She pleaded to her heavenly Father to give her strength for this load of grief.

She thought of her inquisitive, bright-eyed Margriete. She could almost picture her looking after her brothers in her own childish, yet motherly way. She had been such a good helper. But who was calming Margriete's fears? And Pieter, who was now five, the boy who always had so many questions—who was answering his questions now? Nicolas would soon be three. It seemed so hard to believe. Must she actually miss out on his childhood? He was so young. They all were, really. Would Nicolas even remember her? Claudine hated to think of her children grieving for her day after day. Neither could she bear the thought that perhaps they were forgetting her.

When the longings of her mother heart grew almost unbearable, Claudine turned to Jan and showered her affection on him. She had never spent so much exclusive time with any of her other children. But there were no household duties or other children calling for her attention here. And he was such a bright spot in the dreary cell. The jailer had been bringing food for him too, so he was not crying with hunger anymore. Though she knew that nursing Jan increased her own hunger pangs, she would rather endure the hunger herself and see her baby satisfied. She thrilled to see him learn to sit and begin to move around on his own. He must be about six months old now, she figured. It seemed amazing that a baby could develop so normally in a prison cell. True, he was clothed with rags, but she was glad for the rags that they brought her. At least she could keep him covered and clean.

When day followed day in weary succession

and nothing ever changed, discouragement settled like an ominous cloud over Claudine. Always the same four walls keeping her helplessly and hopelessly trapped within. Plenty of time with nothing to do but think. Hours spent thinking about how wonderful it would be to be free. Thinking about those precious family members out there somewhere needing her. Thinking about how easy it would be to recant. Thinking about the hard sufferings she would likely yet have to face. Thinking, thinking, thinking.

But Claudine was wise enough to know that it was the devil's greatest desire to make her despair. So when the cycle of her thoughts became a downward spiral of discouragement, Claudine turned to prayer and song to occupy her thoughts. It became her habit to sing, sometimes for hours at a time until her voice was weak and hoarse. Her fellow prisoners learned to depend on her singing. Sometimes one who was battling loneliness would ask her to sing. At other times they would all sing together.

What would she have done without her fellow prisoners? She wondered if she might not have given up. But it never happened that they all were discouraged at once. There was always someone who could think of something encouraging to share with a despairing companion.

Claudine and Mayken became the best of friends. Both young mothers sharing the same grief, they understood each other. Many hours sped by on wings as they sat and talked, sharing experiences from their past as well as their present hopes and fears.

Anna was another with whom Claudine often shared. She was concerned about this young girl who seemed so troubled and afraid. Claudine tried to draw her closer to God, but it seemed the poor girl constantly struggled.

The day came when Anna and two young men were taken from the cell for questioning. Anxiously Claudine watched them go. The tension and suspense could be felt among the prisoners as they waited quietly and prayerfully for their return. What was happening to them? Would they be faithful?

Claudine was especially concerned about Anna. She recalled her conversation with Anna a few days ago.

"I don't think I could endure being buried alive as they often do with women they put to death. Just thinking about it—being covered up until I couldn't breathe anymore makes me panic. And if they start whipping me or stretching me on the rack, I don't know what I'll do." With quivering voice and tearful eyes, Anna had poured out her burden of fears.

"But listen, Anna," Claudine had encouraged and admonished, "you can't dwell on those thoughts. God will give you the grace to endure if you ask Him to. You know that the Scriptures say that nothing can separate us from the love of Christ."

"I know. I wish I could stop worrying about it. But it scares me. And then there's Herman. I'll probably never get out of here and be able to marry him as we had planned. I can hardly stand the thought that if I am executed, someday he'll probably love and marry someone else." Anna was weeping again at this awful thought.

"God's Word says, 'If any man come to me, and hate not his father, and mother, and wife, and children, and brethren, and sisters, yea, and his own life also, he cannot be my disciple.'[25] I think that includes husbands and future husbands," Claudine had gently reminded her.

"I know," Anna had sighed through her tears.

And now, knowing the young girl's struggles,

Claudine waited tensely and prayerfully for her return. When one young man was brought back alone, with a bleeding back and barely able to walk, the hearts of the prisoners grew heavy with dread.

While Hendrick bathed his bleeding back with water from the bucket that stood faithfully in the corner, the others listened anxiously to what he had to say. It did not take many words to tell the tale.

"The other two recanted under torture."

A new weight of grief settled over Claudine. It was both grief for Anna and a new fear for herself. What if she should do the same thing under torture? She had not experienced that yet. She thought she would not give in, but that nagging fear was there. What if . . . ? "Please, Lord, give me the grace to be true, even in torture" was the prayer on her heart.

The following days were dark for the prisoners. Two who had shared their lot in prison had gone out to enjoy a free world again. The devil whispered that they could do the same. The very thing they did not want to do looked tempting, and they feared they might give in.

Hendrick was, as usual, a great help to Claudine and her fellow prisoners. One day when many were fighting the battles of loneliness, fear, and discouragement, he called them together. "Now, brethren and sisters, we can't let the devil bring us into defeat. Who can think of a song to sing?" The next hours sped swiftly by as the struggling Christians found solace in singing and praying. Once again Claudine's favorite psalm was sung.

The Lord is my light and my salvation;
Whom shall I fear?
The Lord is the strength of my life;
Of whom shall I be afraid?
When the wicked, even mine enemies and my foes,
Came upon me to eat up my flesh,
They stumbled and fell.
Though an host should encamp against me,
My heart shall not fear:
Though war should rise against me,
In this will I be confident.
One thing have I desired of the Lord,
That will I seek after;
That I may dwell in the house of the Lord
All the days of my life,
To behold the beauty of the Lord,
And to enquire in his temple.[26]

Claudine had sung this psalm often before, but it had taken on new meaning here in prison. After the voices of the prisoners were weary with singing, each quoted by turn a promise from the Scriptures. Claudine always greatly enjoyed these times of sharing. The others always would recall and quote passages that she had not been thinking of. It was very refreshing and encouraging.

When her turn came, Claudine repeated with reverence a promise that came clearly to her mind. "For we have not an high priest which cannot be touched with the feeling of our infirmities; but was in all points tempted like as we are, yet without sin. Let us therefore come boldly unto the throne of grace, that we may obtain mercy, and find grace to help in time of need."[27] It was wonderful to know that Jesus, who had Himself died a martyr's death, understood perfectly her struggles. He would give her the strength she needed to be faithful. She would come boldly to Him.

Chapter 11

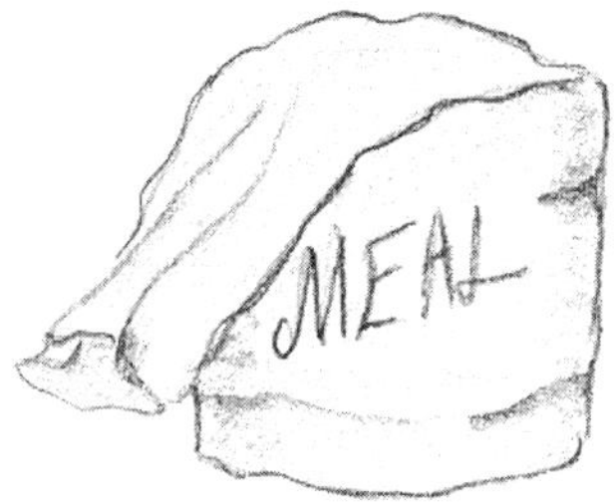

Piersom's strong hands were busy filling a sack with the flour he had just ground, but his mind was busy with other things. He had been here at Ypres for several months, and by this time was familiar with his job and what his employer expected of him. He had been pleased to find work with a miller who was getting older and needed a healthy, strong man to help him. The miller and his wife had even been kind enough to give him meals and lodging in their home as part of his pay.

It was a beautiful place to live, situated on the outskirts of Ypres within sight of the city walls. He wanted to be here at Ypres, close to Claudine. It gave him a certain sense of security to be near the city wall. The stream that ran past the mill and out under the wall provided Piersom with a plan for escape, if he should chance to need one.

The problem that occupied Piersom's mind today was not at all a new one. His mind had been churning this question around for many weeks, ever since he had settled into the routine of life at Ypres. How could he get a message to Claudine? Any mistake on his part would be like setting a trap for himself. But he must get a message to her somehow.

The conversation at noon had intensified Piersom's desire to communicate with Claudine. The miller's wife had been to the marketplace that morning and had walked past the prison on her way. As they ate lunch, she told her husband and Piersom about it.

"I noticed a group of people gathered outside the prison. They were standing along the wall in front of a window. I wondered what they were doing, and as I was about to pass by, I heard a woman singing. I stopped and listened too, and realized it was coming from inside the prison. I could scarcely believe it. I've never heard such beautiful singing, and coming from a prison at that. When I inquired about it, someone in the crowd told me that there's a lady there who's one of those Anabaptists."

Piersom sat motionless, spoon in midair. He was struggling to appear untouched by what the miller's wife was saying. Could that talented singer be his beloved Claudine?

"What I can hardly imagine is that they said she has a baby in there with her." Piersom's sharp intake of breath went unnoticed, for the miller's wife was still talking. "She must be feebleminded! What woman in her normal mind would leave her family and sit in prison just because of religion? Why a woman would be so stubborn and refuse to submit to the state church is beyond me. She must be mixed up in her mind. And that poor innocent baby!" The miller's wife was plainly puzzled.

Piersom bit his lip and absently stirred the food around on his plate. Surely this was Claudine. He was bursting with defenses for her, yet was afraid to speak. What would happen if he would betray himself now? He did not relish the thought of fleeing for his life again. It might be better to keep quiet for the sake of staying close to Claudine.

After thinking a bit, he casually asked, "Could you see the lady through the window?"

"No, I couldn't. It seemed to me that she was down in a deep underground cell, because the window was at ground level and the singing seemed to come from much lower than that."

"Which window was it? Perhaps I could hear her sing myself." There, the question was out. Did it sound innocent enough?

"Oh, let me think. I'm not exactly sure; it's such a big place. One toward the far end; toward the marketplace, I believe it was."

And now as Piersom was busy working, a plan was forming in his mind. He would take a walk this very evening and see if he could discover exactly where his wife was. When he knew that, perhaps he could find a way to get a letter to her. Maybe he could drop it through that window the miller's wife was talking about. He would wait to write any letters though until he could be sure it was his wife, and was sure too of where she was.

Chapter 12

Jan had just awakened from a long and satisfying nap, and he was happy. Claudine set him on her lap and began to chat quietly with him, as she often did.

"You're feeling fine after your nap, aren't you, my little lamb?" Her smile was repaid by an answering smile from her son.

She squeezed him close, and then at his wriggling resistance set him on her lap again. "You are so sweet. You remind me of your father when you smile." A look of pain crossed her face as a stab of longing for Piersom hit her once again. With an effort, she brushed aside the thought and turned her attention back to Jan.

"It won't be long now until our supper comes. Are you hungry too?" As she talked and played with him, he responded with the happy smiles and baby prattle she loved to hear.

"Shall we sing a—" She suddenly stopped short, arrested by a sound coming from the street above. She turned her ear toward the window, straining to hear. The pounding of her heart threatened to drown out the sound. Could it be that that familiar whistle was her husband's? Might he be trying to figure out where she was? The whistling was clearer now. Suddenly it changed to song. Yes! That had to be Piersom!

Claudine burst into singing, her voice quivering with emotion. She sang the first song that came to her mind, the one that so often gave her courage.

> The Lord is my light and my salvation;
> Whom shall I fear?
> The Lord is the strength of my life;
> Of whom shall I be afraid?

Her fellow prisoners looked at her curiously. What had come over Claudine that she should get so emotional and start singing loudly when she had just been playing quietly with Jan?

In shaking, whispered tones she answered their puzzled looks. "That was my husband outside the window whistling and singing. I'm sure of it. He must never have been captured then!"

Sleep was slow in coming that night. Thoughts and questions chased themselves through Claudine's mind. The familiar sound of Piersom's voice had fanned that now-familiar pang of loneliness for her husband into brighter flame. Oh, to see him, to talk with him again, to be sheltered by his care and feel the security of his leadership! How could she ever have taken him for granted? A flood of tears washed her cheeks, and she brushed them quickly away, but more soon followed. It seemed so long since she and Piersom had shared together the normal routines of family life.

She wondered what Piersom was doing. Was he living here in the city, or had he just come to look for her? Did he have the children nearby? At least he was free. She was so grateful for that.

Her mind tossed about for a method to get a letter to Piersom. But, try as she would, she could think of no answer to her dilemma. She did not even have ink or paper to start with.

Pulling her meager garments and her sleeping Jan closer for warmth in the chill night air, she determined to stop thinking in circles and try to sleep. Turning her thoughts heavenward and committing her concerns into her heavenly Father's safekeeping, she finally fell asleep.

Chapter 13

In the dim light of the rising day, Claudine sat thinking. She had awakened early, her thoughts again taken up with the events of the past evening. The sleeping Jan was cuddled close in her arms. She wanted to keep him warm. She had lost track of time, but she could feel the chill of approaching winter in the air.

Once again she was caught by surprise, her thoughts interrupted by that same whistle coming from the street above. She sat motionless for a moment, straining to hear. Then abruptly she plopped Jan down and ran eagerly to stare up toward the barred opening. But those thick walls would allow her no glimpse of the one she loved. Of course she well knew that the wall was so thick that she could not see the street. But in her eagerness, she could not keep from going as close as possible.

Just as the singing drew abreast with the window, Claudine saw something white sail through the air and land at her feet. Exclaiming in surprise and delight, she grabbed it up and hurried over to Jan again. Mayken, who had awakened, looked at her, bewildered.

"It's a letter from my husband!" Claudine whispered in a shaking voice as with hands that also trembled, she unfolded the lengthy letter. A goose quill and a small earthen jar of ink dropped out of the folds of paper. Claudine caught her breath and stared at them in wonder. "Look! He sent these so I can reply!" she exclaimed.

Mayken kindly reached for Jan, who was trying his best to take the letter. He did not often find something interesting to play with. Claudine stepped closer to the window and tilted her letter toward it, straining to see. The room was hushed as she began to read. Those who were awake were keeping one ear tuned for the sound of footsteps in the hall.

Grace, peace, and the joy of Christ Jesus be with you, my dear wife, Claudine, in the Lord. I wish for you, Claudine, a joyful heart and a strong love for God. I want you to know that I remember you night and day with prayers and tears, sighing and praying that God would strengthen you. I pray that He will keep you courageous and strong in the faith continually.

Oh, Claudine, how I reproach myself for leaving you and going to the woods when I knew they were coming for me. I would much rather suffer myself and see you go free. But I have to realize that God allowed things to happen as they did according to His will, and I know I must not fret at what He allowed. I returned to the edge of the woods that day because I was anxious about you, and I saw them leaving with you and our little one on that wagon. After dark, I went to the home of the one who had warned us, and he told me all that happened. He is keeping our household things for us, and he promised to see that the borrowed books would be returned to the place where they belong. I greatly appreciate his kindness.

You remember the young couple who lived next door to us? They took Margriete, Pieter, and Nicolas into their home. I so long to have them with me, but it just isn't possible for the present. They have grieved much for you, my dearest Claudine, but the young wife takes excellent care of them. You know how kind she always was. One thing saddens me though. They have had the children baptized. Although it saddens me, I don't grieve overmuch about it, because in God's sight our little lambs are as innocent as before.

And now, my beloved, I must tell you something that will grieve your heart. I hardly know how to tell you.

A knot of fear tightened in Claudine's heart. What was he trying to say? She was afraid to read on, yet her desire to know all drove her to continue.

Pieter became very ill some weeks ago, and the Lord took him home . . .

Sudden tears blurred the writing, and Claudine could read no further. Propping her arm on the cold stone wall, she buried her face in the crook of her elbow. Such a shock! Could it be?

"Oh, Pieter," she was thinking, "I'm glad you're safe with Jesus now, but what did you suffer before you left? If only I could have been with you to comfort you." How it tugged at her heart to think how he must have wanted and needed her, and she had not been there.

She felt a touch on her shoulder, and then Mayken inquired kindly, "What makes you weep?"

Claudine wiped the tears from her eyes and tried to compose herself. "My little Pieter has gone to heaven." She bit her lip in a vain attempt to hold back more tears as Mayken tried to comfort her.

"Oh, Claudine, I am so sorry. But do not grieve too deeply. He's not homesick for you anymore. And think how happy he is. And he'll never have to suffer what you're going through."

Claudine smiled through her tears. "I know. It's just such a shock. And I can hardly bear to think that I couldn't be with him when he was sick and when he died. I've missed out on so much." Claudine stood lost in thought. Suddenly she realized she still held the unfinished letter in her hand. Raising it, she continued reading.

> . . . and the Lord took him home, where he's safe with Jesus. Oh, my dear wife, I long to comfort you with my presence and to grieve together

with you for our son. I long to ease the shock this surely must be for you. But let us not grieve. He is safe forever. He's not grieving for us anymore, nor will he ever face the suffering you are going through. If he had lived to grow up, perhaps the way would have been too hard, and the enemy too strong, and he would have given up. Now we know he is forever safe and happy with Jesus.

Claudine paused again, still trying to absorb this shocking news. It seemed her dazed senses could hardly grasp it all. Could Pieter really be gone and she had known nothing of it? Numbly she turned to the letter again.

And how is our little Jan faring? I often think of him and wonder if he's getting enough to eat. Are you able to keep him warm? I try to imagine what he might look like by now, and what new things he might be doing.

My dear wife, look to God for your daily strength and comfort. He is able to sustain you. Think often of the Scriptures. I know you have many in your memory that the Lord blessed you with learning. As the Scriptures say, 'Casting all your care upon him; for he careth for you.'[28]

It has done my heart good to write this letter,

and I pray that you will receive it safely and can reply with a letter also. I wonder often how it goes with you and what you may be suffering, and most of all, if you are keeping your courage and faith in God. Remember, Christ says, "The world shall rejoice: and ye shall be sorrowful, but your sorrow shall be turned into joy."[29]

Therefore, dear Claudine, regard not husband or children or anything that is in the world, for Christ instructs His followers, "He that loveth father or mother more than me is not worthy of me: and he that loveth son or daughter more than me is not worthy of me."[30] "For to be carnally minded is death; but to be spiritually minded is life and peace."[31] This is my heart's desire and daily prayer for you, that you can do your best in this.

I want you to know that I am staying not far from you.

Written by your loving husband,
Piersom des Muliers

Claudine tucked the letter inside the folds of her dress, where it would be safe for the present, and reached absent-mindedly for Jan, who was whimpering and begging for her. What a treasure that letter was! She would not have imagined just how much a letter could mean before she had tasted of prison life. And it seemed like such a long, long time since she had talked with Piersom. Now she was bursting with things to tell him. But how?

For the present there were many new things to think about. Pieter. Her mind could hardly grasp the fact that he was gone. She hated to think of that cuddly little body that had been hers to hold now buried in the cold, dark earth. But, no, Pieter was not in that body. He was somewhere in heaven, enjoying a new and much better life. She wanted to try to picture him there, but it was hard to fathom, for she had never been there. A deep longing filled her heart. She wanted to join him there. That would be so wonderful! No suffering, no painful separations. Everything good and peaceful. It was too wonderful to comprehend.

But what about Piersom, Margriete, Nicolas, Jan? She felt torn in two. She could only pray, "Thy will be done in my life or in my death. And thank You for taking Pieter home." She would never wish him back into this miserable world.

Her thoughts turned to the other things Piersom had written. It was just what she needed. Later, in their morning worship, her praise carried a stronger note of joy, spurred by the new courage she had found in reading the heartfelt love and encouragement from Piersom.

Chapter 14

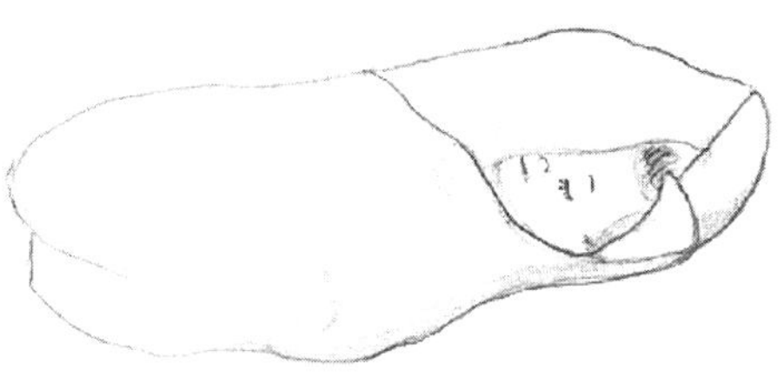

Claudine jerked awake with a start. What had wakened her? She lay motionless, hardly daring to breathe as she listened closely. There it was again, that raspy, grating noise up at the window.

"Mayken, I think someone's filing away the bars from the window." Claudine excitedly jostled her sleeping neighbor.

Others were beginning to stir. Excited whispers filled the room. The minutes seemed like hours as they waited in suspense, half expecting these brave helpers (whoever they were) to be caught at any moment.

In an audible but subdued voice, Hendrick called softly, "Who's there?"

"Never mind who we are. It is better if you do not know. We're getting you out of there if we can. We've already left others out. As soon as we get rid of these bars, we'll throw a rope down for you."

For the prisoners inside, it was almost too good to be true.

But they were not out yet. Tensely they waited, praying, aching to do something to hurry the process, yet helpless for the present.

Suddenly Claudine's excitement vanished, and her heart dropped like lead to her feet. How would she climb a rope with a baby?

Just as that thought struck her, one of the men from the window called, "Here comes the rope. Grab on and climb the wall with your feet while we pull you up."

Soon the first of the prisoners was safely out the window and the next was on his way. Claudine's mind was in a whirl. She and Mayken stood off to one side talking while the others by turn were lifted to freedom.

"Could you tie him into the rope and let them pull him up?" Mayken was trying to think of every possibility.

"But he'd scrape against the wall, and with being wakened from sleep and taken from me, he'd cry and give everyone away. You know how he clings to me, especially if he's just awakened. He'd probably get hurt scraping along the wall and bouncing around in the rope. If only the wall were not so dreadfully high, we could throw him. But it's too dark to see for that." Her voice trailed off as her mind searched frantically for some answer.

Now only Mayken, Claudine, and Hendrick remained in the cell. "Mayken, you go next while we decide what to do about the baby."

Just then a call came from the window. "Hurry, we don't have much time. The guards will soon be changing."

"We've got a mother with a baby that we're not sure how to get up the rope," Hendrick called.

"We soon have to get out of here. You might have to leave the baby and come if you're coming. Hurry!"

"I'll stay here. Mayken, take this letter to Piersom." Claudine had suddenly thought of the letter she had written. Now she could send it to him.

With a choking "God be with you," the two

friends parted, and Mayken soon was out the window and vanished from sight.

"That's all. I'll not leave this sister alone," Hendrick called.

"Are you sure?"

"I am sure." Hendrick's voice was firm.

The last footsteps faded away, and the night was dark and still. The cell seemed strangely empty.

Claudine spoke through the darkness. "Why didn't you go? Surely you're signing your own death sentence by staying here."

"Sister, my conscience would have troubled me if I had gone to my freedom. It would have troubled me to think of you, a young sister, struggling on here alone with your little one. You might have been too sorely tempted and have given up. I could not go. I felt responsible. It does not matter. I'm old and feeble and ready to go to my heavenly Father."

Claudine was both humbled and awed by the unselfishness of this brother in the Lord. She felt at a loss for words. "I don't know how to thank you. May God reward you for your kindness."

She heard Hendrick's footsteps retreating to the far side of the cell, where the men slept, and she groped her way back to Jan, who had slept through it all. Quietly she lay down, but sleep was gone. Her heart was heavy with disappointment. So close to freedom, only to be left behind. Oh, if there had but been more time to think! Maybe they could have worked something out, and she would now be on her way to a glad reunion with Piersom. Oh, cruel thought! She struggled to hold back the sobs as she lay weeping in the now strangely silent room.

She put her arm around the sleeping bundle beside her, so soft and warm. "I couldn't leave you, little one." Then her thoughts took a new despairing turn. "But in the end, if I am executed for my faith, I'll still have to leave Jan." It was not that she had not thought of this before. But it did not lift her spirits to think of it now. Why must it be so difficult to be a mother? Once again, she almost wished she had no children.

She knew she must take her troubles to God. This knot of grief and anxiety was threatening to choke her. "Dear Lord, help me not to get discouraged over being left behind. Give me the strength to go on. And, Lord, keep Your protecting hand over those who are now fleeing. Keep them from being discovered according to

Your will. Bless Hendrick for his kind unselfishness. Heavenly Father, keep Jan and Margriete and Nicolas in Your care. They're Yours, and I commit them unto You. Help me not to worry about the future."

Claudine felt a measure of peace in pouring out her troubles to God. Spent and drained, she fell asleep at last. It seemed she had not slept long when she was awakened in the early morning hours by the scowling jailer. "You are wanted for questioning," he announced to Hendrick.

Hendrick returned some hours later, limping painfully. After the jailer had carefully locked the door and was gone, he explained it all to Claudine.

"They are badly upset about the escape of so many prisoners! I couldn't learn how many are gone, but there are others besides our cell mates. They tried to make me tell who sawed the bars, but I couldn't make them believe that I didn't know. They gave me a brutal beating to make me tell. They can't understand either why I didn't leave."

With a sigh, he sat down painfully on the damp earthen floor. Claudine's heart went out to him. What should she say? She felt responsible, as though it was her fault that he had been whipped and was now suffering.

"Lord, please bless him for his faithfulness" was the thought that echoed through her mind once again.

Chapter 15

Piersom filled his plate with food and reached for a piece of bread. He was not really thinking of his food though. The miller's wife had been to the market this morning, and he was wondering if she would have any news today.

He did not have long to wait. The miller's wife was bursting to report the latest events.

"You couldn't guess what I heard this morning. They say that a good number of those heretics broke out of prison during the night. Someone filed the bars on the windows. The priests and the bailiffs are very upset about it."

Piersom could hardly contain his excitement. He struggled to appear calm. "Did they leave the city? Does anyone know what became of them?"

"No one seems to know. Oh, another thing, that lady with the baby, you know? The one in prison, I mean."

"Yes?" Piersom tensed, waiting anxiously for what was coming. Had she gotten out, only to be recaptured? The thought flashed through his mind.

"They say the only way she could have escaped would have been to leave the baby behind, so she wouldn't go."

Piersom choked, rose abruptly, and headed with quick strides for the door. He could face them no longer. What a disappointment just as his hopes had soared that Claudine might be free!

After a moment, he remembered his uneaten lunch. He should go and finish it, but the thought of food nearly gagged him. Still, the miller's wife so graciously cooked good meals for him, and they would be wondering where he was. Wearily he headed for the house, wondering what he would say to excuse his strange disappearance.

The silence seemed awkward as Piersom took his seat again at the table. Was he hiding his grief from the miller's wife? Her searching gaze seldom missed much. He forced down the tasteless food, and as soon as possible excused himself and headed for the mill again. He was glad the miller lingered behind. He wanted to be alone.

Back in the house, the miller was talking with his wife. "Where did Piersom go during lunch? Was he sick?"

"I surely wondered, but I hated to ask. He seemed pale and quiet when he came back, and I noticed that his hand shook when he ate. Could it be that all this talk about these prisoners bothers him?"

"Maybe you shouldn't talk so much about what you hear," the miller gently chided.

"But he always is so eager to hear it," she defended herself.

"I know."

After thinking a bit, the miller's wife went on. "You know, he's always seemed a little strange. He never told us much about himself, only his name. He seems old enough to have a family, but he's never said anything about a family. He's so thoughtful and pensive at times. Yet he's a very nice man. Makes me wonder if there's some trouble or tragedy in his life." Her voice trailed off.

Back in the mill, Piersom had just begun measuring out wheat to be ground when a shadow darkened the room. Looking up, he saw one of his brethren in the doorway. With a smile, he welcomed him gladly. Here was just what he needed, a brother in the Lord to share his burden.

The brother looked carefully about before reaching into his pocket. Holding a folded packet out to Piersom, he said, "Here is something for you from your wife."

A happy light filled Piersom's eyes, and his smile broadened as he tucked it carefully away for safekeeping.

"Have you heard that a lot of the believers have escaped from prison?"

"Yes, I did." Piersom's smile faded, and a sigh took its place. "Claudine couldn't leave because of Jan. Tell me, do you know, was she the only one left behind?"

"No, they say Brother Hendrick wouldn't leave her behind alone, so he stayed too." Noticing the look of surprise on Piersom's face, he quickly went on. "Brother Hendrick's always been a challenge to me. He's so dedicated to serving the Lord and his fellow men. It's just like him to do something like this, never thinking of himself. Maybe he thought since he's old and doesn't have a family, he is needed more there than anywhere else."

"I would hate to think of her there all alone, with no one to encourage her." A small bit of Piersom's burden was lifted. His visitor was speaking again.

"She sent the letter for you with the others when they escaped. Apparently it was already written."

Piersom felt for the bulge in his pocket, making sure the letter was still safe. It would have to wait until he had the time and privacy to read it.

How that day dragged on endlessly. At last the work was done, and Piersom headed for the house. Refusing supper, he went straight to his room. After hastily lighting a candle, he pulled the letter from his pocket. It was now over six months since he had last seen Claudine. As he opened the letter, even the sight of her familiar neat handwriting touched his heart. Eagerly he drank in the contents of her letter.

"Whom Shall I Fear?"

May grace and peace from our heavenly Father be with you, my dear husband, Piersom. I want to thank you very much for the letter you sent me. It was a great encouragement for me to hear from you.

I had to weep when I read of Pieter's death, grieving because I had not been with him to care for him and to comfort him. But I cannot sorrow too much, for he is happy in heaven, away from all the grief this world holds. Can you think how happy he must be, Piersom? It makes me long to go there.

Jan is doing well, considering his surroundings. The jailer gives me rags to keep him clean and warm, for which I'm very thankful. He also brings food for him, so his needs are met, perhaps better than mine. I thank the Lord for so graciously providing for him.

Sometimes I fear what the future holds for Jan and our other children, but I try to remember that they belong to God and that He is able to provide for them. I have thought that if I am sentenced, perhaps there would be some way to send Jan to you. Have you seen Margriete and Nicolas lately?

My dear husband, I struggle much with loneliness for you and the children, but I can say that God's grace has been sufficient. His promises have become very precious to me, and I find that He keeps them, as the Scriptures say, "The Lord is not slack concerning his promise"[32] and "Let us hold fast the profession of our faith without wavering; (for he is faithful that promised)."[33]

God never promised that we would not face suffering, but He did promise to be with us and bless us if we're faithful. Please pray for me, Piersom, that I can be faithful at all costs. Sometimes the cost seems so high. I wish they would hurry and do something with me rather than just leaving me to sit here for months. I think they know that the long hours are hard to endure.

I am in a cell with eleven others. Two who had been with us recanted. It is very heart-rending to see some give up, and the devil whispers that thus I too could gain my freedom. I shudder to think of the agony and suffering of trying to live with the fact that I had denied my Lord. One of my greatest fears is that I might give in to that temptation in a weak moment. Pray for me that I will be faithful.

I have been questioned, but have not as yet suffered torture, though others around me have. Oh, my dear husband, it seems so hopeless. I had thought that if I would speak the truth, no one could deny it. But their minds are made up, it seems, and they don't even care about what the Scriptures really say. I was questioned on infant baptism, prayers to the saints, the Sacrament, and other things. If they couldn't think of an answer to refute what I said, they would just say that I'm only a woman and can't expect to understand everything. Their whole manner is so haughty and ungodly, and yet they say we are in the wrong.

I must close for lack of space, though my heart longs to pour out many things to you. It has been a real struggle for me, accustomed as I was to sharing my burdens with you and receiving your help and encouragement. Now I must trust in God alone, and He has not failed me.

I pray for you often, my beloved Piersom. I know that it is no small trial for you to think of me here, but please don't blame yourself for escaping when I was captured. God allowed it to be so for a reason, and I am willing to be here, since it is God's plan.

"The Lord is my light and my salvation; whom shall I fear? the Lord is the strength of my life; of whom shall I be afraid?"[34] I always find real comfort in this, and may you find it so with you as well. May God's comfort and peace be in your heart is my prayer for you.

Your loving wife,
Claudine le Vettre

Slowly Piersom folded the letter. He dropped onto the hard wooden floor beside his bed and buried his face in his arms. Oh, words could not begin to express his burdens to the Lord. Something like a groan escaped his lips. The moon was high in the sky before he at last rose from his knees and crawled into bed. But God's peace was in his heart.

Chapter 16

Claudine shifted her position. She had been sitting with her back against the cold stone wall, and she was beginning to feel damp and chilled. It was so difficult to be comfortable in this cell where everything was so hard and cold and unmoving. Just like the hearts of her captors, she thought.

The quietness of the cell today was beginning to grate on her nerves. Just now Hendrick and Jan were both napping, and the silence rang in her ears. She tried to shake off the depressing, morbid thoughts that troubled her, but to no avail. How she missed the captives who had escaped! What was Mayken doing? Was she reunited with her children?

Claudine again envisioned herself returning to her children, hearing happy cries of "Mama!" and feeling little arms wrapped tightly about her neck. How it would thrill her heart to grab those sweet children in a warm embrace. And then to find Piersom, and to weep tears of joy on his shoulder. That would make her happiness complete. The others had gained their freedom without recanting. Why not she? Here she was, still trapped in this prison cell, with little hope of a brighter future. She might as well face it. There was little prospect that the longings of her heart would ever be realized.

Tears rolled down her cheeks and dropped unheeded onto her tattered dress. She felt helpless to stop them. Life looked so hopelessly dark today. Why did God seem so far away? Why did she not feel like praying? Was she after all not a true Christian? As she began to think of all her failings in the past, she sank deeper and deeper into despair.

The fear that had been haunting her the last while added its extra weight to her already sinking heart. She had not been physically tortured yet. When it came, could she cope with that?

Suppose she recanted when the pain got severe? A person does almost anything to get rid of pain. She was sure that she did not want to recant, for if she denied the Lord, would there be hope of forgiveness for her soul? Living unforgiven would be very bleak indeed, even if she were free.

"Sister, what's troubling you?" These words broke into her despairing train of jumbled thoughts. She lifted her eyes still brimming with tears to glance at Hendrick. He had awakened and found her weeping.

Claudine was embarrassed to be caught crying. She did not answer for several minutes as she tried to compose herself and decide where she should begin. For she felt in need of help and was ready for someone to encourage her.

Meanwhile, Hendrick seated himself along the wall not far away. "There is no rush; there's plenty of time here in this place," he was thinking to himself.

"I was just feeling depressed about everything," Claudine admitted brokenly at last. "It's lonely without Mayken and the others. I was thinking of their freedom and wishing for mine too. And when I begin to envision a reunion with my husband and children . . . "

Claudine's voice faltered and, despite her efforts to keep them back, the tears began again. Why must she keep crying? Tears were such embarrassing things, especially in the presence of other people.

"I know that it's extremely difficult because of our deep love for our families." Hendrick paused, and then continued, "But you know, the Bible says, 'He that loveth father or mother more than me is not worthy of me: and he that loveth son or daughter more than me is not worthy of me.' "[35]

Of course! Those words had such a familiar ring. She had thought of them herself at times, and Piersom had reminded her of them as well.

"I know, it's lonely here without those faithful ones who were with us," Hendrick went on. "The devil will try harder than ever now to get us to fall, one way or another. He so often finds his tool of discouragement useful when all else fails." Hendrick's understanding was comforting to Claudine.

"By God's grace, I don't want to let him be successful with me," Claudine responded. "But, oh, the battle looks so hard sometimes," she admitted.

"We don't know what the future holds, so

we should not try to handle it all today. When tomorrow comes with its trials, then God will give grace for them. Never doubt that, Claudine," Hendrick spoke with firm conviction.

Claudine clung desperately to the promise he had given. She wanted to overcome this awful doubt and despair.

" 'Take therefore no thought for the morrow: for the morrow shall take thought for the things of itself. Sufficient unto the day is the evil thereof.'[36] Leave all the tomorrows in God's hand, sister. Maybe Jesus will even return for all of His children tonight. And if not, He has promised to provide all we need. 'My grace is sufficient for thee.' "[37] Hendrick paused again.

"You sound so trusting and sure," Claudine said with a slight smile.

"I'm only sharing what I've learned to cling to through hard struggles myself—just as you now face," he explained. "Here is one more thing for you to think about. When you are tempted to be discouraged, remember, they can only kill the body. That's all. And then your reward in heaven awaits you. Meditate on heaven. It will do you good." Then he quietly moved away, leaving Claudine to ponder the truths he had shared with her.

Heaven. It seemed hard to imagine such a place. No wicked people. How nice! No pain, no hunger, no cold, no sickness. How wonderful! No emotional suffering, no grief, no tears, no partings. And Pieter was there. A smile crossed her face as she lingered on this thought. Little Pieter—did he look like an angel? Was he singing right now? She wished she could picture him, but her understanding was limited. How she longed to go and join him.

But what about Piersom and the children? How marvelous if the whole family could go straight to heaven together!

She knew it was a foolish thought and tried to brush it aside. "But still," she wondered, "could I be truly happy in heaven if Piersom is still enduring the trials of this earth? Oh, well, I can't understand it all, but the Bible promises that we will be perfectly, totally happy in heaven. So however it is, it will be right and good and perfect," she decided.

Yes, heaven was a beautiful thought indeed, but what about the step between? Did an awful death of torture await her? That was not a comforting thought. Then she caught herself as Hendrick's words came to her mind. "Take therefore no thought for the morrow."[38] "My grace is sufficient for thee."[39] Her burden lifted. God would take care of her. She looked down at Jan. The peaceful, contented expression on his face mirrored the peace in her heart.

She began to softly sing,

> In thee, O Lord, do I put my trust:
> Let me never be put to confusion.[40]

Chapter 17

Claudine tensed as she heard the familiar sound of the key in the lock and the rasping groan of the heavy door as it swung open. It seemed she never knew what to expect. Oh, yes, it was just the water boy, coming to fill the bucket in the corner.

The water splashed over the edge as he hastily filled the bucket. Was it Claudine's imagination, or did he seem clumsy and nervous today?

He took a step toward her. Quickly he reached deep into his pocket and pulled out a crumbled letter. "For you" was all he said as he thrust it into her hand and disappeared out the door again.

Claudine blinked in surprised wonder. She had not been expecting this. Glancing toward the closed door, she retreated into a corner. With Jan on her lap, she unfolded the letter, noticing that again there was enough paper for her to reply. Eager little hands reached for the paper, and Claudine plopped Jan on the floor. Eagerly she drank in the message, moving the paper this way and that to keep it out of the reach of Jan's grasping hands. She read,

To my beloved wife, Claudine,

May God's love and peace be in your heart today. Your letter meant much to me, and I thank you for it. It did my heart much good to know that you are remaining true to our Lord. It is my daily prayer that you will continue to be faithful, my dear Claudine.

Others have told me of this opportunity to send a letter to you. I don't want to endanger anyone if this should fall into the wrong hands, but you know of what I am speaking, and perhaps you could reply in the same manner.

I have heard of the escape of the other believers. It was hard for me to accept that you were not able to make your escape too. I have prayed much for you that you would not lose courage, for I am sure that the experience has been a difficult one for you as well. I am glad, for your sake, that the faithful Brother Hendrick is there yet with you. (I have also heard about this.)

O Claudine, I wonder continually what you are facing and suffering. Be faithful, and you will receive a heavenly reward that will be worth all the suffering. Jesus has promised, "My grace is sufficient for thee: for my strength is made perfect in weakness."[41]

Claudine had received strength from this promise before, but it encouraged her once again. She knew all too well how weak she was in her own strength, but Jesus was promising her His strength.

Although and because I love you very deeply, I would not want you to purchase your freedom at the price of your faith. Think of the unhappiness and suffering that that would bring you.

I have been to see Margriete and Nicolas. Margriete has a greater struggle than Nicolas with grieving for you, for she understands more. But they are being well taken care of. It's hard for me to leave them, for they cling to me piteously. I pray for them much, as I know you do too. At times I can't help but be glad that our Pieter is happy in the presence of the Lord.

My much-beloved wife, I urge you to be valiant, "looking unto Jesus the author and finisher of our faith; who for the joy that was set before him endured the cross, despising the shame."[42] Paul says, "Yea, and all that will live godly in Christ Jesus shall suffer persecution."[43] Think about Hebrews chapter eleven. I am sure that with your excellent memory of the Scriptures, you can recall it. It speaks of so many righteous witnesses, who through their faith suffered much, having respect unto the recompense of their reward. "They were stoned, they were sawn asunder . . . were slain with the sword . . ."[44] You are not alone in your suffering. "Wherefore seeing we also are compassed about with so great a cloud of witnesses, let us lay aside every weight, and the sin which doth so easily beset us, and let us run with patience the race that is set before us, looking unto Jesus the author and finisher of our faith,"[45] as I wrote once before in this letter.

May God comfort, strengthen, encourage, and bless you abundantly. Fight valiantly, and you will receive the reward of the righteous.

Written by me, your husband and brother in the Lord,

Piersom

Claudine folded the letter thoughtfully. Piersom perhaps would never know just how much his letters gave her renewed courage.

But sometimes they brought with them fresh grief for her children. At times she could not help but wonder, "Why, Lord? Why must innocent children suffer so?" She longed with all her being to go to them, dry their tears, quiet their fears, hold them close, and promise them that she would never leave them again. *Never.* But that was not hers to say.

The burden on her heart grew heavier as she pondered the awful questions, "Will my children grow up to follow the right path? Who will teach them?"

"Dear Lord, help me to bear this struggle. Please, Father, be with my children. Touch their lives with peace; guide their feet into the right path. Comfort their lonely hearts. If they're not going to serve You when they grow up, take them to glory now in their innocence." She hoped that was not a selfish prayer. She knew that she could not have prayed that quite so freely had she been with them.

She thought of her little son already walking on golden streets, and a tearful smile erased the pain on her face. Would his feet have been prone to wander on the wrong paths? The mischievous, fun-loving Pieter was forever safe with Jesus. No tears for Mother, no longings for Father, no pain, no fear . . . She could not wish him back to this ugly world. "Oh, Pieter, will you know me when I get there? I wish you could tell me now what it's like."

But her thoughts inevitably returned to her motherless children trying to cope with a cruel, ugly world. "Why?" her mother heart cried. Guiltily she stopped herself. "I must not ask why." Yet the question persisted.

As she groped for an answer, she seemed to hear Jesus' words when on earth, "Suffer the little children to come unto me, and forbid them not."[46] Jesus had taken time for the little ones, and He could watch over hers too. Had He not said that the heavenly Father sees each sparrow that falls? Surely He cared for her children much more than for the sparrows. If He could feed the birds and clothe the flowers, could He not provide for her children? Desperately she clung to these threads of comfort.

Stirring from her reverie, she folded the letter and tucked it away. Finally, taking notice of Jan, who was clamoring for attention, she stood him on her lap and held his hands.

Perhaps it was the letter that stirred Claudine's impatience. Later that day she said to Hendrick, "I'm so weary of sitting here day after day and month after month. I'm not suffering torture, but doing nothing can be tormenting too. I've been sitting here all winter, and spring has arrived again. It was a hot August day when I came," she recalled.

"They know that time will break a person down. That's why we have to fill our minds with prayer and the Scriptures. Don't give in to boredom and discouragement," Hendrick replied.

Knowing this was true, Claudine tried to think of something to sing. From a corner of her memory, she pulled out a song that she had memorized from *Het Offer des Heeren.* It was a lengthy song, telling of the suffering and victorious death of a sister in the Lord some years before. Softly she began to sing:

She was a maid of tender limbs,
    Elizabeth her name was given;

"Whom Shall I Fear?"

The handsome town in which she lived
    Was known as Leeuwarden.

'Twas January she was seized,
    In fifteen hundred forty-nine;
Her eager loyalty to Christ
    Brought her to be in jail confined.

They brought her to the prison house
    Where they compelled the youthful maid
To swear according to the law
    If she as yet a husband had.

When hearing this she answered them,
    "To swear an oath I never can;
With nay and yea we answer you,
    No, lords, I live not with a man."

"They say you are a teacher that
    The souls of many men mislead.
Now give the names of all the ones
    To whom you taught your unsound creed."

"Oh, no, my lords, let me in peace;
    I never will their names expose,
But ask about my faith in God."
    She answered frankly, well-composed.

"Whom Shall I Fear?"

"What do you think about the Mass,
    The worthy Sacrament as well?"
"About these things I cannot find
    That anywhere the Scriptures tell.

"About the Supper of the Lord,
    However, I have often read,"
She said, referring to the night
    Christ passed the cup and broke the bread.

She quoted much the Word of God,
    To which in faith she closely clung.
Her captors thus accused her, saying,
    "The devil has possessed your tongue."

"The servant," she replied, "is not
    Above his master's level." *True,*
Thought she, *My Lord was falsely blamed*
    Of having had a devil too.

"Tell us, is child baptism wrong
    And not of any value then?
We know that you're in favor of
    The sect that baptizes again."

"My baptism as a helpless child
    Has never met my greatest need,

As did believer's baptism when
    On God in faith I did believe."

"Can priests forgive the sins of men?"
    "No, lords, how could I ever show
That Christ as Priest alone forgives
    If to the priest instead I go?"

Succeeding this with short delay,
    They brought her out and led her soon
Unto the executioner
    Inside the dreaded torture room.

"Till now we have examined you
    With goodness and with gentle care,
But you would not cooperate;
    Now we will start to be severe."

They placed two thumbscrews on her hands
    (With lingering pain she'd surely quail)
And crushed her thumbs and fingers till
    The blood gushed from her fingernails.

"Oh, I just cannot bear the pain."
    "Confess your wrong, and we will stay."
"Help me, O Lord," she said with tears.
    "Oh, be my helper, God, today."

"Whom Shall I Fear?"

"Confess. Confess," they called to her,
"For then we will decrease your pain;
Again we say to you, confess;
Don't quickly call on God again."

She cried to God most fervently,
Who heard and made her pain abate.
She calmly said, "Now question me;
The pain no longer is so great."

They put two screws into her shins.
"Don't shame me thus," she cried at that.
"No man has ever known me so
Nor touched my being when so unclad."

With this she fainted in their hands;
They thought that maybe she was dead.
But she awoke within her bonds.
"I live; I am not dead," she said.

"And will you now take back the words
That you before have spoken here?"
"No," answered she, "I'll seal it, though
Through death I make the token clear."

In March of fifteen forty-nine
Her final sentence was disclosed;

But she with godly courage brave
Could not be quickly discomposed.

She faced her death by drowning with
A trust that shows unto us all
That when we cry in pain and hurt
The Lord will hear our every call.

—Translated by Irvin B. Horst
—Versified by Joanna Hursh

The above song follows in the Dutch language.

Twas een maechdeken van teder leden
Elisabeth dat was haren naem
De welcke was woonachtich ter steden
Van Leeuwerden een Stede bequaem.

In Januario wert sy geuangen
Het was int vijftienhonderste Jaer
Negenenveertich, sy had verlangen
Nae Christum. Dien sij beleet aldaer.

Men brachtse opt Brockhuys in corter wijle
Daer hebben sy haer ghedrongen an
By haer eedt te seggen, na swets stijle
Ofte sy niet hadde eenen Man.

"Whom Shall I Fear?"

Sij heeft geantwoort, als sy dit hoorden
Te sweeren ons geensins betaemt
Ja in, neen neen, sullen zijn ons woorden
Ick en ben met geenen man versaemt.

Men seyt als dat ghy verleyt veel lieden
En dat ghy ooe een leeraersse zijt
Dus wilmen dat ghy sult bedieden
Wie ghy geleert hebt in v tijt.

Och neen mijn Heeren laet my met vreden
Van desen, en vraecht na mijn geloof
Geern wil ick v daer van geuen reden
Heeft sy gesproocken voor blint en doof.

Mer wat ist dat ghy hout van die misse
Ende dat hoochweerdige sacrament
Van sulex en las ick noyt yet gewisse
Mer wel van sheeren Auontmael ient.

Sy sprac so veel schrifts ter seluer stonde
Dat sy aldaer seyden int gerecht
De Duyuel die spreect wt uwen monde
Ja niet meer dan zijn Heer is de knecht.

Segt den kinderdoop mach die niet vromen
Dat ghy v wederom doopen liet

"Whom Shall I Fear?"

Neen niet weer ben ick daer toe gecomen
Alst eens op mijn geloof was geschiet.

Mogen die Priesters oock sondt vergeuen
Neen sy, hoe soud ick geloouen soo
Christus deenige Priester verheuen
Die alleen reynicht ons van sonden snoo.

Daer na sonder lange te verbeyden
Brachten sy Lijsbet weer voor den Raet
En mits dien lieten sy haer doen leyden
In den pijnkelder voor den Hencker quaet.

Wy hebben v noch alleen tot huyden
Niet dan met goedicheyt aengegaen
Mer wilt ghy ous vraghen niet beduyden
Met hardicheyt willen wy bestaen.

Sy lieten haer twee duym ijsers setten
Als sy niet wilde lijden in lanck
So dat sy duym en vingeren pletten
Datter tbloet ter nagelen wt spranck.

Och ick en macht niet langer verdragen
Belijdt, men sal verlichten v pijn
Helpt my o Heere, sprac sy met clagen
Want ghy zijt eenen noothelper fijn.

"Whom Shall I Fear?"

Belijdt, belijdt, riepen sy ter zijden
So salmen v doen verlichten wel
Want wy seggen v van te belijden
En niet van te roepen tot God snel.

Maer sy hielt al aen tot God seer vuerich
Die haer verlichte, en sy sprac coel
Wilt my nv vry voort vragen geduerich
Want ick als voren geen pijn en voel.

Noch twee scroeuen setten si op haer schenen
Beschaemt my niet, heeft sy doen geseyt
Want van eenich mannen my noch genen
Sijn hant aen mijn bloot lijf heeft geleyt.

Mits dien beswijmde sy onder de handen
Datmen seyde sy is doot by geual
Mer sy ontwect zijnde in de banden
Sprac, ic ben niet doot maer leef noch al.

En wilt ghi dat noch niet spreecken tegen
Het welc ghy voor ons bekent hebt hier
Neen ick, sprac sy tot haer onuerslegen
Mer wilt met mijn doot besegelen fier.

In Martio in den Jare voorsproocken
Gaf ouer haer een oordeel den Raet

Met drencken hebben sy haer ghewroken
    Aen dat lief Schaepken, die Woluen quaet.

Och laet ons aenmercken metter herten
    Elisabeths mannelijck gemoet
Wanneer sy ter noot leet pijn en smerten
    Heeft aengeroepen den Heere goet.

Chapter 18

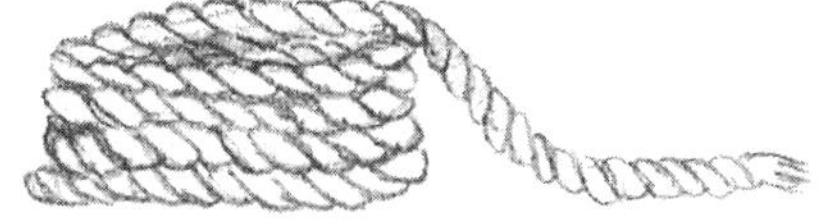

The morning of this warm spring day had been damp and chilly, but by afternoon the cell seemed more comfortable, though it was always damp and cool. Claudine stood Jan on the floor, stooping to hold his small hands in her bigger ones.

Making happy little noises, Jan hesitantly stepped out, clinging tightly to his mother's hands. His little bare feet took wobbly steps on the uneven earthen floor. They had gone halfway across the spacious cell when Claudine heard the key turning in the lock. Quickly lifting Jan, she placed him on one hip and turned with trepidation to face the door.

The heavy door groaned open. In the doorway stood the jailer, a length of rope in one hand. "You are wanted for questioning," he addressed Claudine in his usual blunt, crude manner. "Come with me."

Hendrick stepped forward. "I'll keep Jan here," he offered, reaching out to take the little boy. Not at all pleased, Jan set up a loud wail.

While the jailer tied Claudine's hands, Hendrick walked to the far side of the room, trying his best to pacify the crying boy.

As Claudine was led away, the wails of her baby echoing from the dungeon rang in her ears and tore at her heart. She had nothing to do all day but play with him, and he had come to love his mother dearly.

As she was led down the hall and up the stairs, her womanly dignity recoiled at being seen as she was. She tried in vain to brush back the matted, unruly hair that escaped from under her stained and crushed covering. Just as futile were her attempts to brush the wrinkles and smudges from her dress. She knew she was filthy and smelly. She, who had always loathed dirt, now had to look like this! "I must bear even this for Christ's sake," she told herself.

Mounting the last step, she followed the jailer as he led her into a nearby room. Feeling weak and breathless from climbing the stairs, she sank gratefully down onto the stool that was shoved toward her. The jailer left the room.

Looking about her, Claudine recognized one of the priests who had questioned her before. Several others were seated with him at a long table. Her eyes rested on one man who sat staring at her idly. He held a quill in one hand poised over a stack of papers, his chin resting on the other hand. She supposed he was the clerk of the criminal court. Two other men completed the group. One she recognized as the magistrate, and the other bore the dignity of a judge.

The magistrate cleared his throat. "You have had ample time to consider your ways. We wanted to give you plenty of time." His smile was cold and repulsive. "Are you now ready to confess your sins to the priest, and return to your family, where you ought to be?"

Claudine responded quietly, "I know of no sin to confess."

"Come, now," he chided, "surely you're not perfect. You've been here all these months, and you've never made any confessions, and you say you've nothing to confess?"

"The priests cannot forgive sins anyway. Only Christ can forgive sins. I confess my sins to Him."

The magistrate raised his hand. "Stop. Don't you ever show such disrespect to this learned man"—he pointed to the priest—"whom I have brought to win your soul."

Now the priest began to speak. "We are sorry that you have embraced this foolish opinion. I would not honor it enough to call it a faith. It's just an opinion." The priest spoke in a degrading voice.

Claudine answered with firm conviction. "We desire to do only what Christ in His Word teaches us. We want no part with your idols and temples, nor your commandments of men. Stephen once said that 'the most High dwelleth not in temples made with hands.' "[47]

"You foolish woman," he declared in disgust. "What, in the name of our holy mother, do you mean about idols?"

"Do you not have many idols of wood and stone, and images of silver and gold? The Scriptures plainly say, 'Take ye therefore good heed unto yourselves . . . , lest ye corrupt yourselves, and make you a graven image.' "[48]

"How you do twist the Scriptures. Since you think the priests cannot forgive sins, let me teach you what the Scriptures say. Did not Christ say to Peter, 'Feed my sheep'[49] and that upon him He would build His church? And did He not give Peter the keys of heaven and all priestly authority to loose sins or retain them?[50] And do not the holy popes sit on the same seat and have the same authority? For they are successors of St. Peter. What do you say now to that? Let us hear."

"Christ said that upon this rock, meaning Peter's confession of faith in Him, He would build the church. He said nothing about popes, or successors, or priestly authority to forgive sins."

"But He did speak of the keys of heaven and loosing and binding. And if there were no pope or priests, then who, pray tell, would have the authority to absolve and forgive sins?"

"Christ is our only Mediator. The whole Book of Hebrews plainly teaches us that."

"You foolish woman. How can you act like you know so much of the Scriptures? At what university did you study?" The priest sneered at her. "I studied divinity at the university for years, and yet you claim to know better than I what the Scriptures say."

Suddenly to Claudine's mind came a fitting reply. "In Matthew 11:25 Jesus said, 'I thank thee, O Father, Lord of heaven and earth, because thou hast hid these things from the wise and prudent, and hast revealed them unto babes.' "

"Of course," he said drily. "God reveals His truth to cobblers, lanterntinkers, broom makers, millers, thatchers, and all sorts of lousy beggars, and even to the women. And to us ecclesiastics who have studied for years, He hides it. Listen to this woman talk! You Anabaptists can't tell *A* from *B* before you are baptized, and suddenly, as soon as you are baptized, you can read and write. I tell you, there's something strange about this."

"You must not think it strange that the grace of God helps our young believers when we diligently teach them to read."

"So you presume to have the grace of God. Don't you know that St. James teaches the sacrament of confession?"

"In James it says, 'Confess your faults one to another.'[51] If I would confess my faults to you, would you confess yours to me?" Claudine wondered.

"You proud Anabaptist, who do you think you are, anyway, to say that the holy priests must confess to you? Such blasphemy!"

Claudine looked calmly into his glaring eyes, and the priest looked away.

In a quieter tone he began again. "Christ Himself said, 'Go shew yourselves unto the priests.'[52] Now what can you say?" Folding his hands together, he fixed his accusing gaze upon her.

Claudine was calm and quick with her answer. "Jesus said that to the lepers He had just healed. They were to show the priests that they were clean. He said nothing about confessing sins. They had to show themselves to the priests to get permission to go among the people again, from whom they had been separated because of their leprosy. That was part of the Jewish Law," Claudine explained.

"Oh, bah, it says plainly, 'Go and confess to the priests,' for so our mother, the Holy Roman Catholic Church, understands it." The priest spoke with determined finality.

Claudine made no reply. What was the use in arguing?

"See, you have nothing to say. You're in a corner now," the priest jeered. With a rustle of his priestly robes, he leaned forward and started in again, leaving no chance for Claudine to reply. "Now tell us, you Anabaptist"—he spat out the word as if it were poison itself—"who is your husband?"

Claudine did not immediately reply. Was this a trap? Surely they knew who her husband was. Were they prying for information on his whereabouts? "You know who my husband is, I think," she replied.

"Oh, we do? We know you filthy Anabaptists. Your men have the women in common and run together just like the dogs. Isn't that a fine thing?"

Claudine's cheeks flushed at such talk. She felt her temper rise hot within and breathed a prayer for calmness. With steady voice she replied, "That is not true. We are slandered in this."

"You are a lying woman!" the priest stormed. "You would deny this, but it's true. They certainly were Anabaptists who took the city of Muenster by force and held it for a time. And they did have all things common, including the women. They robbed churches and convents too. And you want to deny this? I suppose you thought I didn't know of this, but it's true." He glared at her insolently.

"Those were false teachers. We want no part in any of their wickedness. They are not our brethren." Claudine wanted that part clearly understood.

"You can try to deny it as much as you like, but I still know it's true." The priest shut his mouth firmly, as if that settled the matter.

The magistrate cleared his throat. "Where is your husband?"

"I don't know." Claudine was so glad she could truthfully say this.

"Woman, I do not believe that you know nothing at all of his whereabouts. Where is he?" he asked with particular emphasis on his last three words.

"I do not wish to tell you anything. You would only use it to his hurt." Claudine sat in determined silence, watching the clerk busily writing down all that was said.

"We can make you tell." The magistrate nodded menacingly while he glared at her. "Have you received word from him?" He sat watching her very closely, as though trying to read her mind. Those steely eyes seemed to bore straight through her.

What should she say? She pondered for a

moment. Again she said, "I do not wish to tell you anything."

Inwardly Claudine was trembling and praying for strength. To be questioned concerning her faith was one thing, but to be used to gain information about other brethren—this was frightening. She in no way wanted to be responsible for the capture of her husband or anyone else. In the back of her mind lurked the fear of torture. Would they torture her if she refused to tell what they wanted to know? "Lord, keep the door of my lips and give me a clear mind to think carefully."

As she had guessed, this was only the beginning of their terrible prying.

"Where was your baby born?"

"In Meenen."

"Was your baby baptized?"

"There was no need for it."

"Humph! Listen to her foolishness," the priest inserted.

"And who attended the birth of that child of yours?"

"A midwife friend of ours."

"But who is this friend?"

"I do not wish to tell you."

"We shall make you tell!" The magistrate

was becoming incensed. The barrage of questions went on and on without their gaining the answers they hoped for.

"Who baptized you?"

Claudine had decided she could answer this one. Leenaert Bouwens had not been in these parts for several years, and it could do him no harm.

But they were not satisfied.

"Who was present?"

"Where was it done?"

"Who were your leaders in Meenen?"

"Where were your meetings held?"

Claudine would tell them nothing.

Finally, in disgust, the magistrate rose to his feet. "You stubborn and foolish woman, perhaps you will be more ready to change your foolish notions and answer our questions if we take you to the next room and show you the things we have to help you see your foolishness. You know, we've helped a lot of people that way."

Chapter 19

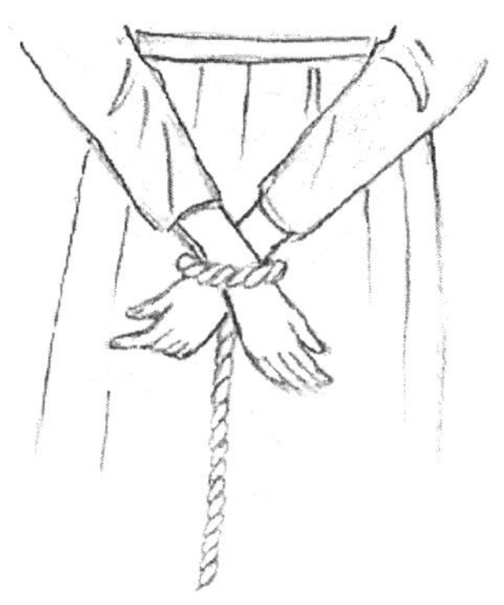

As in a dream, Claudine allowed herself to be led by her roped hands to what she knew would be the torture room. She felt strangely calm as she contemplated in those few brief moments what might befall her. "I will be faithful," she determined. "Keep my tongue, Lord."

She glanced around. There was the rack, the first thing to catch her gaze. It resembled a table with ropes at each end and at one end a crank. Then off to one side, seated by a fireplace, she spied a tough, burly fellow, looking generally unkempt. He ceased scraping the dying coals together and gazed at the latest specimen brought in. On a table near him lay an assortment of things strewn about—whips, screws, tongs, weights, ropes, and the like.

The dark, dreary room was an altogether unlovely place. On the floor around a post in the center of the room, Claudine saw what she suspected to be bloodstains. That must be the whipping post. She would have succumbed to the horror and panic rising within her had she not called on God for strength.

The magistrate was speaking. "Now you see, we can ask this man to assist us if you still refuse to cooperate. Are you willing to reconsider your ways and submit to our Holy Roman Catholic Church?"

"I can do nothing but what Christ and the Bible teach me, and it teaches me that I cannot be a part of your idolatrous Catholic Church." Clear and firm came Claudine's reply.

With a shrug of his shoulders, he motioned to the executioner. "Perhaps you can help her."

Claudine was tossed ruthlessly onto the rack. Lying flat on her back, she shut her eyes in prayer. She made no resistance as her hands and feet were tied securely. The executioner began to crank.

Claudine could feel her body stretch longer

and longer. The pain mounted with every crank. It streaked through her wrists, her arms, her legs, her ankles. She could not help but groan in utter agony. Something would surely snap soon.

The magistrate was standing over her. "Just tell us you recant, and we'll let you free."

Claudine shook her head. The burning, searing pain was awful, but for Christ's sake and by His grace she would bear it.

The magistrate tried again. "Tell us where your husband is, and we'll stop this. I know that you know something."

She clenched her teeth and shook her head. "Lord, help me. Help me!" Her inward cry ascended over and over to the throne of the Almighty, and she sensed her Lord's nearness.

"Crank until she speaks," in frustration the magistrate harshly commanded.

The pain grew unbearable. Suddenly a scream escaped her lips, and then merciful blackness enveloped her.

Chapter 20

Jan was crying. Claudine struggled to wake up. She blinked her eyes and started to sit up. Oh, why did she hurt all over? Helplessly she flopped back again. Looking about, she spied Hendrick holding Jan, who was crying and holding out both arms toward his mother.

The fog began to clear, and suddenly she remembered—she had been racked! What a relief to be back here and not still on that awful rack. But how did she get here? She did not remember coming back to the cell. She felt too weary to think. And, oh, how she ached all over.

She must comfort Jan. Claudine struggled

again to sit up, but the pain was too intense. It seemed that every joint must be out of place. Finally, with Hendrick's help, she managed to sit up. Painfully she reached to take Jan, only to realize that her racked limbs could not support his weight. Hendrick kindly placed him on her lap.

After Jan had been pacified, Claudine spoke. "Did they carry me back?"

"Yes. So you've been racked." It was not really a question; he already knew the answer.

Claudine nodded, shuddering at the memory. "They tried to make me recant, and also to tell where Piersom is. I wouldn't tell them, and then I must have passed out."

As the days passed, Claudine's pain gradually subsided. Soon she could walk again and move more easily, but she was quiet and withdrawn as she pondered her situation. Somehow she sensed that this was only the beginning of her sufferings. Was the end drawing near? Many times she wished she knew. Within her breast raged a constant battle between fear of the future and trust in her Lord.

"Can I handle more suffering? What if I recant under torture?" The fear was very real.

" 'My grace is sufficient for thee.' "[53]

"But what if I in my weakness let some information slip? What if I reveal something that I did not intend to? What if I should be the cause for someone else's suffering?"

" 'But when they deliver you up, take no thought how or what ye shall speak: for it shall be given you in that same hour what ye shall speak.' "[54]

"What if they kill me? Many others have already died." The fear of execution loomed like a great giant before her. She loved life. She did not really want to die now. And yet, she did not want to go on living if life was not God's will for her. Yes, it would be wonderful to be in heaven, but, oh, the road between!

Then she remembered her Saviour. What was it He had said when He looked death in the face? " 'If it be possible, let this cup pass from me: nevertheless not as I will, but as thou wilt.' "[55]

Tears burned her eyes. To think that Jesus must have felt just as she was feeling! "He understands! He knows how I feel!" How wonderful were the words of the Scriptures. Every time fear threatened to swallow her up, a treasured promise would come to her mind, one that she could cling to and that brought rest.

Many were the desperate prayers that reached the ears of the heavenly Father, and Claudine sensed that her prayers were heard. The battle was not easy, but His grace was sufficient.

Chapter 21

Not many days had passed when Claudine was once again called for questioning. As she painfully climbed the long flight of stairs, she wondered how she would return.

She was taken to the torture room and given a seat. The same now-familiar faces surrounded her.

The magistrate began in a kind voice. "I'm expecting you to be wise and willing to cooperate now. We don't like to deal so harshly with women, but if you don't confess, we have no choice. We will be happy to let you return to your family and forget all this. Would you not like to do that?" His mouth spread into a beguiling smile, but his eyes were cold and hard.

Unsure of his meaning and not wanting to trap herself, Claudine simply looked at him with questioning eyes.

Not getting a reply, the magistrate went on. "Surely by now you've seen the foolishness of your strange notions. You should be able to see the wrong you are guilty of. You are not filling your proper place as a mother. You are disobedient to the church and to the laws of our country that command you to be an obedient member of the Holy Catholic Church. Are you now ready to confess your guilt in this as a good citizen should?"

"I am a citizen of the heavenly country, and the Scriptures say, 'We ought to obey God rather than men.'[56] I am willing to obey in anything that is not contrary to God and His Word. The Catholic Church I cannot be a part of, because it is not a true church."

Much incensed by this reply, the magistrate spoke with icy firmness. "I see you still persist in your foolishness. We shall make you submit. We have ways of doing it." He nodded significantly. All gentleness gone in an instant, he suddenly was harsh and businesslike. "We'll not put up with your foolishness forever, you know. You've only begun to taste of our methods, so you might as well give in now and save yourself. King Philip II is tired of all this nonsense with you foolish people, and his governor, the Duke of Alva, won't waste his time with you either. He's already gotten rid of a lot of troublemakers."

Yes, Claudine had heard of the Duke of Alva and his "Blood Council." Such news traveled, even seeping through prison walls. Under the orders of the king, the Duke of Alva had been sent to the North to bring order. He was not hesitating to use any method to stamp out heresy. His council had rightly earned its popular name, "The Blood Council."

The magistrate was speaking. "Do you know what happens to people like you who persist in this foolishness?"

"I know that you put them to death. You'll have to give an account before God for that someday," Claudine replied.

"We do the world a favor. We are only ridding the world of troublemakers" was his cruel and undaunted reply. Then getting on with the business at hand, he said, "Now answer my questions properly, and we'll soon be through."

Then followed the same questions she had heard before, questions she refused to answer.

"Where is Piersom?"

"Who are your leaders?"

"Who attended the birth of your baby?"

"Where were your meetings held?"

To all of this, Claudine refused to give any information. She would only say, "I cannot tell you."

At last, in anger and frustration, the magistrate said, "Give her a taste of the whip. Then perhaps she'll speak."

The executioner came forward. With experienced speed, he tied her fast to the whipping post.

Claudine closed her eyes in prayer, waiting for the blows to fall. She gasped as the first cruel lashes rained down. She staggered and would have fallen had she not been tied. Over and over the torturous whip whistled and fell. Would it never end? The fire in her back was unbearable. At last, panting and exhausted, the executioner threw down his whip. He slowly untied the ropes until Claudine dropped unsupported to the floor.

Through her dazed senses came the hard sound of the magistrate's voice. "Perhaps now she will learn."

Claudine was roughly lifted to her feet and placed on a nearby chair. She prayed for strength to remain true under such excruciating pain. The thought struck her that Jesus had endured this very kind of treatment for her sake, and knowing this strengthened her courage.

"Now what do you have to tell us?" the magistrate asked.

"Nothing."

"Just say you'll recant, and we'll let you go."

"I will adhere to Christ and His teachings."

No amount of begging, threatening, pleading, or arguing could change Claudine's mind. She would confess nothing. She would reveal nothing.

At long last, she was led limping back to her cell, weary and spent. An anxious Jan was delighted to see her. Hendrick, too, was glad to see her and to know she had been faithful. The hours had been long, filled with prayers for Claudine and attempts at keeping Jan happy. He knew so well what she was going through. He was facing these very experiences himself.

Claudine was glad when the day drew to a close and she could put Jan to sleep for the night. Her pain-racked body could hardly bear the lively antics of her busy boy. He was learning to take a few wobbly steps and unless he was sleeping, was never still. This evening he had wanted to climb all over her in glad rejoicing that she was back. Oh, the pain he innocently brought to her fresh wounds.

There was little sleep for Claudine's aching body that night. At times she tried to pull the shreds of her dress loose from the dried blood, where the whip had torn her flesh.

Unnoticed in the dark night, many tears washed Claudine's cheeks. Why must the battle be so hard? Mingled with the pain of the fresh wounds from her lashing was the constant pain in her heart for her loved ones. It seemed her circumstance would be easier to bear if Piersom would be here to help her bear it, to soothe her wounds, and to encourage her. Yet she would never wish for him to be in this awful place.

As she turned to God in prayer, she found comfort in pouring out all her fears and woes to God. Somehow, as she prayed, heaven seemed to draw nearer.

Heaven—a place of no tears, no sufferings, no heartaches, no evil; a place in the presence of Christ and the Father. Pieter was there. Never had she longed to go there as she did now.

Suddenly a new realization dawned upon her. This suffering was doing something good for her! It was making her long for heaven in a way she never had before!

Chapter 22

The long, painful night finally gave way to gray dawn. Claudine faced the new day soberly. What would this day bring forth for her? More suffering?

Though she had no Bible now, she always liked to begin the day with God. Before Jan would awaken to distract her thoughts and occupy her time, she would quote Scriptures and pray.

This morning, as usual, she spent some time in meditation, though it seemed that that was what she had done all night. As she tried to remember God's promises, her mind felt foggy and blank. What was wrong? Hunger, suffering, and the strain of everything were taking their toll on her memory. As she realized this, a new wave of despair threatened to engulf her. "Lord, how can I be faithful if I can't remember Your promises?"

Jan was stirring. He sat up, rubbing his eyes and looking around expectantly. A glad smile lightened his face at the sight of Claudine, and he held up both little arms.

Gingerly, cautiously Claudine reached to pick him up. Squeezing him close, she kissed his soft cheeks. "Little one, you're so irresistible when you ask to be held like that." Wrapping his arms about her neck, he laid his head on her shoulder, completely content and secure.

After breakfast, once again the jailer appeared. "I am to take you and the baby upstairs," he said with careful emphasis.

Fear shot like a dagger through her heart. What did this mean? What would they do to Jan to try to make her give up?

Hendrick's face revealed his grave concern and sympathy. "I'll pray, sister," he promised quietly.

Claudine was trembling as she bravely forced her aching body up that long flight of stairs.

"Please, Lord, spare me. I can't take much more," she thought. The jailer had to carry Jan, though she could hardly bear to give him up. Somehow, instinctively, she wanted to cling fiercely to him and never let him go.

She breathed an inward sigh of relief when she was not taken to the torture chamber, but rather to the room where she had been questioned before.

With Jan on her lap again, she turned her attention to the magistrate and the priest before her.

"Will you confess your error and obey the church as a good citizen should?"

"I know of no error to confess."

"But you know that you have not obeyed the mandates of our Holy Catholic Church; will you admit that?"

"I admit that I refuse to be a part of your idolatrous worship, for it is not the true faith that Christ teaches."

"And in what way is it idolatry?" the magistrate's voice challenged coolly.

Claudine sighed. Oh, where should she begin? After thinking a moment, she started carefully. She noticed the clerk, with hand poised, ready to write down every word she said.

"You have many idols. You have your crucifixes and your images. You pray to Mary and many other dead saints. You take the bones of the dead and place them in chests or on altars. All this is not needed. I believe the Word of God says, 'Thou shalt worship the Lord thy God, and him only shalt thou serve.'[57] 'God is a Spirit: and they that worship him must worship him in spirit and in truth.'[58]

"Since God dwells within the true child of God, we have no need nor is it right to pray to images and dead saints, or to confess to priests. All our prayers and confessions should be to God, and when we have wronged our fellow men we should confess that wrong to them.

"Jesus said, 'Come unto me, all ye that labour and are heavy laden, and I will give you rest.'[59] Also, it is written, speaking of Jesus, 'Neither is there salvation in any other: for there is none other name under heaven given among men, whereby we must be saved.'[60] You see, this is why I cannot pray to Mary. She was just another person like me. She cannot do anything for me, as you believe."

Claudine stopped, somewhat surprised at having made such a long speech. The words had simply bubbled out, aided by the Holy Spirit and carried by the strength of her firm conviction and faith in God.

"Tush, tush! Don't give such disgraceful slander against our Holy Mother Mary. A country woman like you can't be expected to understand everything."

Claudine was completely weary of their poor answers. Just when she was sure that they would *have* to understand what she was saying, they would scold and treat her like a fool or a simpleton.

The magistrate now changed the subject. "You have already confessed that you have been rebaptized. Were you not afraid of the authorities?"

"I fear God more than the authorities."

"Claudine, it will go hard for you if you do not submit to mercy for your misdeeds."

"I know of no misdeeds that I am guilty of in the eyes of God."

"But do you not believe that the Scriptures teach, 'Obey them that have the rule over you?'[61] and 'Honour the king?' "[62]

"Yes, I believe that. I also must add that I, like our persecuted forefathers, believe that I must obey God rather than men. I will obey the laws of our country in all things except where they defy God's laws."

"Do you not know that the king has decreed death to all who have been rebaptized?"

"Yes, I know that."

"Yet you still persist in your foolishness." He shook his head in disgust and frustration. Turning to the priest, he said, "You must prove to her that she is wrong."

Clearing his throat and licking his lips, the priest began with a great torrent of words. Claudine listened, outwardly patient, but inwardly weary of going over the same things, when she was convinced in her heart that God and truth were on her side and were not with her accusers. Jan too must have been weary of it, for he began to fuss and squirm.

When Claudine was given a chance to speak, she began, "It's no use. I know that I have a peace and joy in my heart that I never had in your church. I cannot damn my soul by submitting to your demands. Do with me as you wish; I will be faithful to my Lord." Conviction rang in her voice.

One priest sputtered in anger. "Your suffering will only begin when we're through with you. The devils will deal with you then with fire and brimstone."

Claudine spoke quietly. "I'm glad you're not the Judge of all the earth. The Scriptures say, 'Be not afraid of them that kill the body, and after that have no more that they can do.' "[63]

The magistrate spoke up. "So will you in no case listen to us and give up your rebellious ways?"

"I will give up any rebellious ways that I know myself to be guilty of."

He shook his head. With lips set in a grim line he rose. He walked to the door of the room and called for the jailer. With pounding heart, Claudine wondered what was about to happen. It did not appear that he was through with her, yet why was he calling the jailer?

The magistrate returned to stand before Claudine, glowering fiercely down at her. Two pairs of eyes looked up at him, one innocent and the other troubled. "That child," he said, pointing a long finger at Jan. "Have you ever considered what would happen to him if you persist in your foolishness?"

Claudine felt small and helpless under his stern gaze. She wanted to take Jan and run, anywhere, anywhere to get out of this awful place. She was shaking. What did this mean? "Please, please, Lord." The silent, imploring cry echoed in her frightened thoughts. Instinctively she held Jan tighter, and he looked up at her with questioning eyes.

The magistrate was waiting for an answer.

"I—I had thought if I am sentenced, perhaps I could send him to my family," she finally ventured.

"Oh, you did!" The magistrate's lip curled in a sneer of contempt. "We're giving you a choice today. Give up your faith or your child. The choice is yours. Which will you give up?"

Claudine's face blanched. Those words were like horrible blows, worse than the lashes that had lacerated her back. She bowed her head over the tousled head of her little son and squeezed him close. "I can't give Jan up . . . But I can't give up the faith!" She sat, dry-eyed and stunned. "Lord, Lord, spare me, please!"

The magistrate's voice came again, harsh and cruel. "Shall we take the baby, or are you willing to submit?"

Claudine could only shake her head. Oh, the turmoil inside! One voice was screaming, "Give up the faith," while another was imploring, "But you can't do that!"

Again that cold, cruel voice spoke. "Will you confess your error? If you don't, we'll take that child and give him to someone who will give him proper training. We do not want him to grow up to be rebellious as you are. Will you confess your sin?"

Claudine's mind was reeling. This was for real. They had told her to bring Jan. The jailer had been called. "Jan, Jan, I can't let you go! But, oh, I cannot, cannot give up the faith."

Once more the magistrate spoke. "You must answer me now. Will you submit and confess your mistake?"

With eyes now brimming with tears, Claudine looked up. "I can't, sir," she cried out in anguish, "but, oh, sir, please, please, have mercy!" Her baby was clasped to her breast.

"Take it," the magistrate ordered the jailer.

Footsteps came near, and Jan was torn from her arms. As his frightened cries faded away, Claudine's tears gave way to shaking sobs. Every muscle of her body ordered her to follow the jailer and plead for her son, yet she sat unmoving.

The magistrate was in front of her. He thought he was close to victory. "You can have him back if you'll only give up," he said in an almost-soothing tone.

Claudine would only shake her bowed head

to all his begging and pleading and promises. She simply could not give up her faith. It was not possible.

At last she was led back to the cell with empty arms and red, swollen eyes still brimming with tears.

Chapter 23

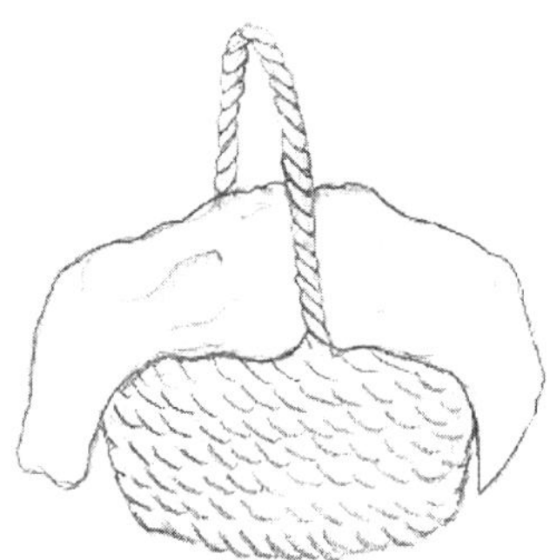

Side by side, Piersom and the miller strode to the house. The sun stood high in the sky, shedding its warm rays over the countryside. Tempting smells welcomed the hungry men as they reached the door of the miller's home.

The miller's wife was hurrying about. She did not want to keep the men waiting. "I should have had dinner ready sooner. I must confess that I loitered a bit in the marketplace this morning."

Her husband chuckled. "You like to talk, don't you?" he said with a teasing grin.

"I wasn't gossiping," she asserted. Growing

serious, she went on. "There was talk again of that lady in the prison. She still sticks stubbornly to her notions, no matter what they do, so they took her baby now to try to persuade her."

A smitten look flashed across Piersom's face. "What did they do with it?" He had to know the answer to this awful question.

The miller's wife looked curiously at the suddenly pale, anxious man before her, waiting so intently for her answer.

Piersom tried to calm himself.

"Well, they gave him to someone who will train him to obey the church, of course."

"But did anyone know who has him?" Piersom could not disguise the anxiety in his voice.

"Of course they won't tell that." Again she eyed him curiously. "But come, let's eat. Dinner is ready." She pulled out her chair to sit down.

"Will you please excuse me? I'm not hungry today." Piersom choked out the words and disappeared, not waiting for a reply.

Left to themselves, the miller and his wife began to eat. "What ails him? He always gets so upset if there's bad news about that lady in prison."

The miller was puzzled. "You really should not mention her, Mother."

"But he always wants to hear. You know he does," she defended herself. "I just can't figure him out. Why should a strong man let himself get so upset over these stubborn people in prison? It's their own fault if they have to suffer."

The miller said nothing as he put a bite of food into his mouth.

"Maybe he's just a very softhearted man. He's always been kind and gentle," his wife said meditatively.

With bowed head and heavy heart, Piersom walked back to the mill. Finding a quiet corner, he let the tears flow. It seemed too much to endure, thinking of his wife in that awful dungeon, suffering untold grief over this new pain.

"Oh, Jan!" his heart cried out. "Lord, how can You allow this? Pieter is safe in heaven. That grief is small compared to this. Is Jan doomed to grow up, never knowing of our faith in God? Lord, give Claudine strength to handle this awful grief."

Anguished thoughts raced through Piersom's dazed mind as he struggled to accept this new blow. Then in his jumbled thoughts a plan began to take form. He must do something. He must talk to someone. He would try to find out what had become of Jan. There was no way he could stay in this mill all afternoon and hide his burden.

After splashing cold water on his face, he walked with purposeful strides toward the house. Taking a deep breath, he forced himself to walk in and speak to the miller. "May I have the afternoon off? I have some business I would like to attend to."

The miller scratched his head, thinking for a moment. "Yes, that should be all right. I think I can handle it myself this afternoon."

Late that night, Piersom sat down in his room. By the light of the candle, he began a letter to Claudine.

> May God's abiding love and comfort be with you in this hour. This is my heartfelt longing for you, my chosen wife.
>
> I want you to know that I have heard about Jan being taken from you. I have tried to find out where he was taken, but I have learned nothing. They don't want anyone to know this.
>
> It brings me much grief and sorrow of heart, especially when I think of you there in the prison,

sorely tempted and grieving. I know what anguish this must bring to you, for I know how dearly you love all of our children.

I can hardly bear the thought of Jan being placed in the hands of strangers. Who will teach him to fear the Lord? Oh, my dear Claudine, I can scarcely write to you for the tears that want to come.

Take heart, and keep the faith. Paul says, "For I reckon that the sufferings of this present time are not worthy to be compared with the glory which shall be revealed in us."[64]

"For we know that if our earthly house of this tabernacle were dissolved, we have a building of God, an house not made with hands, eternal in the heavens."[65] "And God shall wipe away all tears from their eyes; and there shall be no more death, neither sorrow, nor crying, neither shall there be any more pain: for the former things are passed away."[66]

Think on this, Claudine. There will be no tears, no sorrow in heaven. That's my desire and prayer for you. I'm beginning to wish for you the glories of heaven. As much as I love you and long to see you, I do not wish to have you return to me having given up the faith.

I want to share with you the things that give me a measure of comfort when I think of Jan. The

Scriptures say, "Lo, children are an heritage of the Lord."[67] Jan belongs to God. He gave him to us, and now He has allowed him to be taken away. Herewith we must commend him to the Lord, who is able to watch over him. We must pray that God will spare him and protect him. "The effectual fervent prayer of a righteous man availeth much."[68]

I know that you love your family deeply from the heart and that there is no reason under heaven for which you would voluntarily leave them. But for Christ's sake, it has been forced upon you. We have never been assured of a permanent life together here on earth. We all must die and be separated someday.

Do not think that it is easy for me that our family has been separated. I write these things to encourage myself as well as you in this great trial. Think of Job and all the ways that the devil used to try to make him curse God. "The Lord gave, and the Lord hath taken away; blessed be the name of the Lord. In all this Job sinned not, nor charged God foolishly."[69] This is my constant prayer, that you can have such a faith as Job had.

I would gladly take your place in the dungeon. Indeed, I think at times that it would be easier for me to bear your pain myself than the suffering I endure when I think of you being there. But God has allowed it to be as it is; this I must accept.

My dearest Claudine, I am thankful to the Lord for the years He permitted us to be together. I'm sorry for the times I failed to be a good husband to you, and I thank you for being a faithful and wonderful wife to me. If I never see you again in this life, I trust to meet you again in heaven. These are dangerous and uncertain times. None of us has a promise of tomorrow.

Greet the brother who is with you, in my name. I would greatly rejoice to hear from you and to know how you stand, but I trust and pray that you can be of good cheer in the Lord.

I will remind you yet of your favorite psalm. "The Lord is my light and my salvation; whom shall I fear? the Lord is the strength of my life; of whom shall I be afraid?"[70]

Written by me, Piersom des Muliers,
Your husband and brother in the Lord

With a sigh, Piersom laid down his quill. He picked up the letter and reread it. Oh, it was so difficult to know how to encourage Claudine when his own heart was bleeding. Perhaps he had not disclosed just how great his grief was. The letter sounded more courageous than he felt at times. Yet he was determined to cling to those words of comfort that he had given her. And, somehow, writing comfort to her had been a balm for his own soul. He could only pray that it would do the same for her.

Chapter 24

Another long day had begun. Claudine sat quietly along the wall, letting her mind wander.

It was so hard to know how to fill the long hours with anything other than thinking. And always her thoughts wanted to turn to Jan. What was he doing now? She pictured him waking up in someone else's home and being cared for by a stranger. Where was he? Was he wanted and loved? Would they treat him well? Was he still crying for her, or had he forgotten her? She was sure he soon would forget, if he had not already.

Oh, the agony of it all. Jan could forget, but she could not. Would she never stop crying? She had never realized how much Jan had filled her days with cheer and comfort until now. Now he was gone. Time seemed to stand still. One endless day followed another in weary, monotonous succession.

The hardest battle was thinking of Jan's future. Would he grow up not knowing the paths of the Lord; never knowing the faith of his father and mother? Oh, if he should be doomed to miss heaven, what was the use of keeping on?

As these terrible thoughts pressed in upon her, they made her sink lower and lower into despair. Why not just give up? She could at least be a mother to her family and point them to the right way.

The racking and whipping had been easier to take than this. Why should she go on to be faithful and reach the blissful, painless, glorious world of heaven, when her family would be left behind, fragmented, motherless, and perhaps left to the mercy of unbelievers?

It was terrible to be left here alone—sitting day after day, thinking about Jan and missing his sweet, bubbling innocence; sitting with aching arms, with no one to fill them and nothing to occupy them through the long, long days; nothing to do but think, think, think. She knew that her persecutors intended it to be this way. They had guessed rightly that it would be the most difficult thing she could face.

But she could pray. Countless were the hours she spent in prayer, many times with tears streaming down her face. Those hours in prayer helped her to keep on. At times the comforting presence of Jesus seemed so real. Here in this cell she had learned to know Him and trust Him as never before. Though her grief did not disappear, yet she knew a settled peace. Her God was with her.

With a voice that trembled at times, she sang to occupy her thoughts. As she sang song after song that she had memorized from her martyr book, she realized that she was not alone. Other mothers and fathers had walked this difficult road. God had helped them to be faithful to the end. They had calmly and cheerfully gone to their deaths, eager to move on to their home in heaven. Desperately she prayed that God would give her calmness and good cheer as well.

No, she could not, she dare not give up. If she did recant, what kind of mother would she be? What kind of wife would she be? It seemed impossible to try to go on living without God. She could not live without praying and telling

God her troubles. What would she do when one day she did face death? To whom could she turn without God? No, there was no way she could give up the faith. Life without God would be more bleak than this prison cell.

But, oh, the flesh was so weak. "Must I never see my children again? Never see their childish smiles? Never hear their little voices telling stories so important to them? Leave them to someone else to train and to watch them grow up?

"And my beloved husband. At least he is a man, capable of being responsible for himself. But must our marriage be forever over? There are no marriages in heaven." Gone from her mind were the memories of mistakes. She remembered only the blessed times, the special joys they had shared together.

Piersom's letter was like a light in a dark night. Yes, he was right. She would be true to Christ at all costs. She must. There was no other way. Deep in her heart, she loved the Lord and wanted to be faithful, but the temptations were so real. Yet she knew what she must do. Her love for Christ must come before all else.

One dark day, a phrase from the Scriptures suddenly came to Claudine's mind. Did it not say something about a mother forgetting her sucking child? She searched through her memory, trying to recall just how it was. Piece by piece, it came back to her. "Can a woman forget her sucking child, that she should not have compassion on the son of her womb? yea, they may forget, yet will I not forget thee."[71]

Claudine's fears and worries melted away. Glad tears washed her cheeks. Could it really be true, that God cared about her even more than she cared about Jan? She could hardly fathom it. As impossible as it would be for her to forget Jan, it was even more impossible for God to forget her. Her heart swelled with love for her Lord. If He could not forget her, He would not forget Jan either. "Lord, help me to remember that Your ways are higher than my ways. I do not understand now why all this grief must be, but someday perhaps I will." She rebuked herself for not trusting her heavenly Father more.

What would she do without faithful Brother Hendrick? Though weak and battered from the sufferings he himself endured, yet he did his best to encourage Claudine. His strong faith was a constant challenge to her. When the burden grew too heavy, she knew she had only to share it, and he would help her to think of some truth that she could cling to and find rest.

Hendrick had reminded her that every person must give an account for himself alone before God. Her children would be accountable for themselves one day, if they lived to grow to the age of being able to understand and choose for themselves. And God would be fair, for He is a just God. She too was responsible to answer before God for herself alone. She must leave Jan's future and the future of each of her children in God's hand. As she thought on this, she knew it was true.

As the days passed, her prayers took on a new dimension. She was growing tired and weary. "Lord, I pray that You will give me courage and strength to resist this temptation of the flesh. I am willing to offer myself as a sacrifice for You. I know that I am weak, and I pray that You might soon deliver me from these trials." Many times she prayed this prayer, asking God to bring her trials to an end.

She felt within herself that probably she would never be released. She fully expected to die a martyr's death. One nagging thought that troubled her voiced itself in her prayers. "Father, if I am sentenced to be executed, I ask that You will take away all my fears so that I can go cheerfully and calmly to my death. I want You to receive all glory, in my life or in my death." She did not want to go to her death weeping or frightened and shaking. She wanted to be able to go calmly, knowing that God was with her.

"Wouldn't it be wonderful if someone else would come to know and serve the Lord through my death?" she mused.

Chapter 25

Piersom faced the new day with a heavy heart. He felt drained, spent, utterly exhausted. He had passed a sleepless night. He had prayed until there were no more words to say. He had wept a flood of tears. His mind had thought of countless things.

Today was the day that Claudine would die. The Duke of Alva had ordered the prisons to be cleared of heretics.

As the morning light streamed in through the window, he pulled out Claudine's last letter to him. This would have to satisfy his intense longing to talk with her. He had received this letter not many days ago, and surely she had not changed her mind since then.

Yes, the letter reassured him, she was determined to be true, even to death, which she fully expected.

Once more he knelt in silent petition for his wife before leaving his room to face the realities of this day. How could he go through the normal routines of the day when his wife, his own beloved wife, would be cruelly put to death today?

Piersom knew he would not be able to go and watch his wife's execution. It would be too much to endure to see her burning. The horrors of his imagination in the night hours had been bad enough. Difficult as it would be, he would have to pass the morning hours somehow. Tense from his sleepless, night-long vigil of thinking and praying, he decided he might as well work.

Stepping into the kitchen, he attempted a cheerful "Good morning." The miller's wife looked up from stirring the porridge to return his greeting.

Piersom forced himself to eat a few bites of the morning meal. He needed strength for the day. The miller's wife hurried busily about, putting things in order.

"Piersom," she said, "I'm going this morning to see the execution of that lady. I can't imagine what kind of person would be so stubborn. I must see her for myself. Would you like to go with me and watch too?"

Piersom cleared his throat. "No, I don't care to see it. But will you watch carefully and tell me all about everything when you get home?"

"Yes, certainly I will. I must be going now, for I want to be there early." Slipping into her wooden shoes and placing her market basket on her arm, she bustled out the door and started up the street.

The long morning crept by slowly for Piersom. Prayerfully he went about his work, getting little done. His thoughts were too distracted for him to function well. He breathed a sigh of relief when the noon hour at last arrived.

Piersom walked toward the house with the miller, anxious to hear what the miller's wife would have to say, yet dreading it. How could he endure such a horrible tale? Yet he must know how Claudine had taken it all.

He studied the miller's wife anxiously. She did not wait long to begin her story.

"Piersom, you should have been with me

this morning," she said to him. "I went to the prison first of all. A group of people stood outside the prison, and we heard them come for Claudine (that was her name) to take her to her execution. When they told her what they had come for, she started singing. It was so beautiful, and she sounded so happy. I just don't understand it. She must not have had a normal mind to understand what they were saying; that's all I can think," the miller's wife said with a puzzled shake of her head.

"She sang, 'The Lord is my light . . . ; whom shall I fear?' Someone said that that is a psalm in the Bible."

"Did you see her executed?" Piersom was anxious to know the full story.

"Yes. We followed them as they took her and a man named Hendrick to the marketplace to be executed. They both seemed so happy and content. You would have thought they were going to a wedding or a supper. Their hands were tied and their mouths gagged. If they had not been gagged, I'm sure Claudine would have been singing. I've never seen anyone so happy. Her eyes just shone." The miller's wife was disturbed by it all. Dinner was forgotten as she went on with her story.

"When we reached the place of execution, there was a scaffold already set up. Two stakes were there with wood piled around them. The executioner put Claudine and the man on the scaffold and tied them to the stakes. Then he strangled them. They stood there so quietly and willingly." Her voice began to tremble and her eyes filled with tears.

Feeling embarrassed, she quickly brushed the tears away and cleared her throat. "I don't know why it affects me like this. They seemed so happy and innocent. If they just wouldn't have been so stubborn," she said.

"While they were being tied to the stake, Claudine closed her eyes and raised her tied hands toward heaven. I suppose she was praying. She looked so calm and joyful and peaceful." The miller's wife shook her head again. She was baffled by it all. "When she was strangled, she didn't fight it. It seemed like she just fell asleep. Then they burnt them."

The story was finished.

"I cannot understand why such nice people would be so stubborn," the miller's wife repeated again in genuine bewilderment.

Piersom could control his emotions no longer. This time he made no attempt to flee as the tears flowed from his eyes. It was such a relief to hear that Claudine had been faithful, and to know that now her sufferings were over. He would tell his friends the truth regardless of the consequences.

When he could control his voice, he spoke. "That was my beloved and very rational wife whom you saw executed this morning."

The miller and his wife were astonished. "What?" The miller's wife could not believe she had heard correctly. Feeling weak, she sat down on a chair and gazed at Piersom with open mouth.

"That was my wife, and she was in her right mind," Piersom said again. A firm determination to defend the truth erased all fear and feelings of grief for the present. "I share the same beliefs that she has given her life for."

The miller and his wife could hardly grasp yet another piece of shocking news. They were speechless.

"When she was arrested, the Inquisitors were coming for me, but I escaped, and they took her. I came to this town because my wife was here in prison."

The pieces were beginning to fit together for his listeners. No wonder Piersom had seemed so disturbed by the stories the miller's wife carried home.

"Why do you not support the state church?" The miller asked the question. He and his wife were ready to listen. Dinner was completely forgotten.

Piersom seated himself at the table, and the miller followed his example. Piersom breathed a prayer for wisdom. Where should he begin? He looked at the miller's wife. "You told us how happy and peaceful my wife was. God gave her that peace and happiness because she obeyed His Word and trusted in Him. The state church does not obey the Word and has no peace with God to give.

"Besides," Piersom continued, "there are so many practices in the state church that are entirely contrary to the Scriptures. We try to follow only what God's Word teaches. It is for these reasons that we were not and I am not a part of the state church."

Piersom excused himself and hurried to get his Bible. He returned to his seat and began turning through the familiar, well-worn pages.

"You see," he explained, "we never found true peace in confessing our sins to the priests. In the Old Testament times, before Christ came, the priests were necessary in God's plan to offer sacrifices to God for the people. But in Hebrews we read that Jesus' death on the cross marked the beginning of a new and better covenant.

"In order to obtain salvation, we must come to Jesus. It is He who has died for our sins, and He is our only Mediator. Let me read to you from Hebrews. 'We are sanctified through the offering of the body of Jesus Christ once for all.'[72] In the Catholic Church we were taught that each Mass is Jesus' bodily presence on the altar being offered to God by the church for an atonement for man's sin. But you see according to God's Word here, that is false, for this verse says that Jesus' body was offered for the sins of the people 'once for all.' Let me read more.

" 'And every priest standeth daily ministering and offering oftentimes the same sacrifices, which can never take away sins: but this man, after he had offered one sacrifice for sins for ever, sat down on the right hand of God.' "[73]

Piersom paused and looked up. "It's wonderful to know that He is there today, being our Mediator to God. We can come boldly and directly to Him in prayer without going to a priest, and He hears us.

"In one place the Scriptures say, 'Wherefore

come out from among them, and be ye separate, saith the Lord, and touch not the unclean thing.'[74] The Bible teaches us that we have to be separated from what is sinful and wrong if we want God's favor.

"You know yourselves how evil some of the priests are. You know how many illegitimate children there are in our towns, fathered by the priests who have taken a vow not to marry. Surely you know that such as that is sin. And many more evils are practiced and tolerated in the state church."

Slowly the miller and his wife nodded their heads. Yes, they understood what Piersom was saying.

"You perhaps know that we are called Anabaptists." He paused and looked at them questioningly. Again they nodded.

"The reason for that is this. The Scriptures say, 'He that believeth and is baptized shall be saved.'[75] These are Jesus' own words. Can a baby believe?"

Together, the miller and his wife answered, "No."

"In the Scriptures we find adults, not infants, being baptized. When Claudine and I realized our need, we confessed our sins directly to God in the Name of Jesus, our Mediator, trusting God to forgive our sins. We were then baptized upon the confession of our faith in Him."

Piersom watched his audience closely, and, yes, they seemed to be comprehending the truth of what he was saying.

"The Scriptures say," he continued, " 'Thou shalt worship the Lord thy God, and him only shalt thou serve.'[76] In another place it says, 'God is a Spirit: and they that worship him must worship him in spirit and in truth.'[77] Paul in his writings warns us to 'flee from idolatry.'[78] Our faith is in Jesus Christ alone, not in relics, saints, or Mary. We worship nothing and no one but Christ and the Father."

The miller spoke. "I knew that some of the things we've been taught didn't make sense, but I never realized exactly what the Bible says about them. But doesn't the Bible say that we should obey them that have the rule over us? If we're commanded to be part of the state church, I thought that we have to obey."

"But the Scriptures say too, 'We ought to obey God rather than men,' "[79] Piersom replied. "If the commands of the state defy the commands of God, then I must obey God first."

The miller's wife spoke hesitantly. "She

certainly went to her death peacefully. She was not afraid at all. I couldn't have done that. She must have had something we don't have."

Piersom nodded vigorously. "She had the peace that only Christ can give. The Scriptures promise that 'all that will live godly in Christ Jesus shall suffer persecution.'[80] But God also promised, 'My grace is sufficient for thee.'[81]

"Our sufferings have not been easy, but I wouldn't trade an easy life for the assurance of having Christ in my heart and the peace that He gives. I'd rather have a free and pure conscience and a hope of heaven than to have an easy life here and torment in the next. That was Claudine's choice too, and that hope kept her faithful to God and His truth till the end."

On and on they talked. Piersom read many things from the Scriptures, and the miller and his wife listened carefully. The hours flew by unnoticed.

The sun was sinking into the western sky when the miller said brokenly, "I wish to have the peace that your wife died with."

His wife had only been waiting for him to say it first. "Oh, I long for that too," she cried.

"Are you aware of what it might cost?" Piersom cautioned. "It could cost you your lives, just as it did my wife. It will not be an easy life, but I can promise you God's peace."

"I could die tomorrow from some other cause, and I know in my heart that I would be afraid to die. I want to be ready to face God in peace as your wife was," said the miller's wife.

The angels in heaven rejoiced as the miller, his wife, and Piersom knelt in prayer. Two souls had found salvation in Jesus Christ.

THE END

Epilogue

This story about Piersom and Claudine is based on the account in *Martyrs Mirror* (pages 737, 738). Much of the information about the times in which they lived was taken from *Anabaptism in Flanders 1530–1650* (Herald Press). Most of the characters in the story are real.

The questionings were adapted largely from the record of various questionings throughout *Martyrs Mirror*.

The family was never able to find out what happened to Jan. The miller and his wife were baptized, and soon afterwards they too joined the ranks of the martyrs.

Persecution against the Mennists (Mennonites) in Flanders continued for many years. Many migrated north to Holland. They were practically nonexistent in Flanders by 1650.

Endnote References

1. Matthew 5:39.
2. Hebrews 13:5.
3. 2 Corinthians 12:9.
4. 1 Peter 5:14.
5. 1 John 4:4.
6. Matthew 5:11, 12.
7. 1 Peter 3:14–17.
8. 1 Corinthians 10:12.
9. Ephesians 6:11–15.
10. John 18:36.
11. 1 Corinthians 10:14.
12. Acts 2:38.
13. 2 Corinthians 6:14–18.
14. 2 Corinthians 5:17.
15. Matthew 10:29.
16. Romans 12:19.
17. Psalm 27:1.
18. 1 John 4:4.
19. Romans 8:35–39.
20. Luke 12:11, 12.
21. Luke 22:19.
22. 1 Timothy 2:5.
23. John 8:51.
24. Luke 16:19–31.
25. Luke 14:26.
26. Psalm 27:1–4.
27. Hebrews 4:15, 16.
28. 1 Peter 5:7.
29. John 16:20.
30. Matthew 10:37.
31. Romans 8:6.
32. 2 Peter 3:9.
33. Hebrews 10:23.
34. Psalm 27:1.
35. Matthew 10:37.
36. Matthew 6:34.
37. 2 Corinthians 12:9.
38. Matthew 6:34.
39. 2 Corinthians 12:9.
40. Psalm 71:1.
41. 2 Corinthians 12:9.
42. Hebrews 12:2.
43. 2 Timothy 3:12.
44. Hebrews 11:37.
45. Hebrews 12:1, 2.
46. Mark 10:14.
47. Acts 7:48.
48. Deuteronomy 4:15, 16.
49. John 21:15–17.
50. Matthew 16:18 19.

51. James 5:16.
52. Luke 17:14.
53. 2 Corinthians 12:9.
54. Matthew 10:19.
55. Matthew 26:39.
56. Acts 5:29.
57. Matthew 4:10.
58. John 4:24.
59. Matthew 11:28.
60. Acts 4:12.
61. Hebrews 13:17.
62. 1 Peter 2:17.
63. Luke 12:4.
64. Romans 8:18.
65. 2 Corinthians 5:1.
66. Revelation 21:4.
67. Psalm 127:3.
68. James 5:16.
69. Job 1:21, 22.
70. Psalm 27:1.
71. Isaiah 49:15.
72. Hebrews 10:10.
73. Hebrews 10:11, 12.
74. 2 Corinthians 6:17.
75. Mark 16:16.
76. Matthew 4:10.
77. John 4:24.
78. 1 Corinthians 10:14.
79. Acts 5:29.
80. 2 Timothy 3:12.
81. 2 Corinthians 12:9.

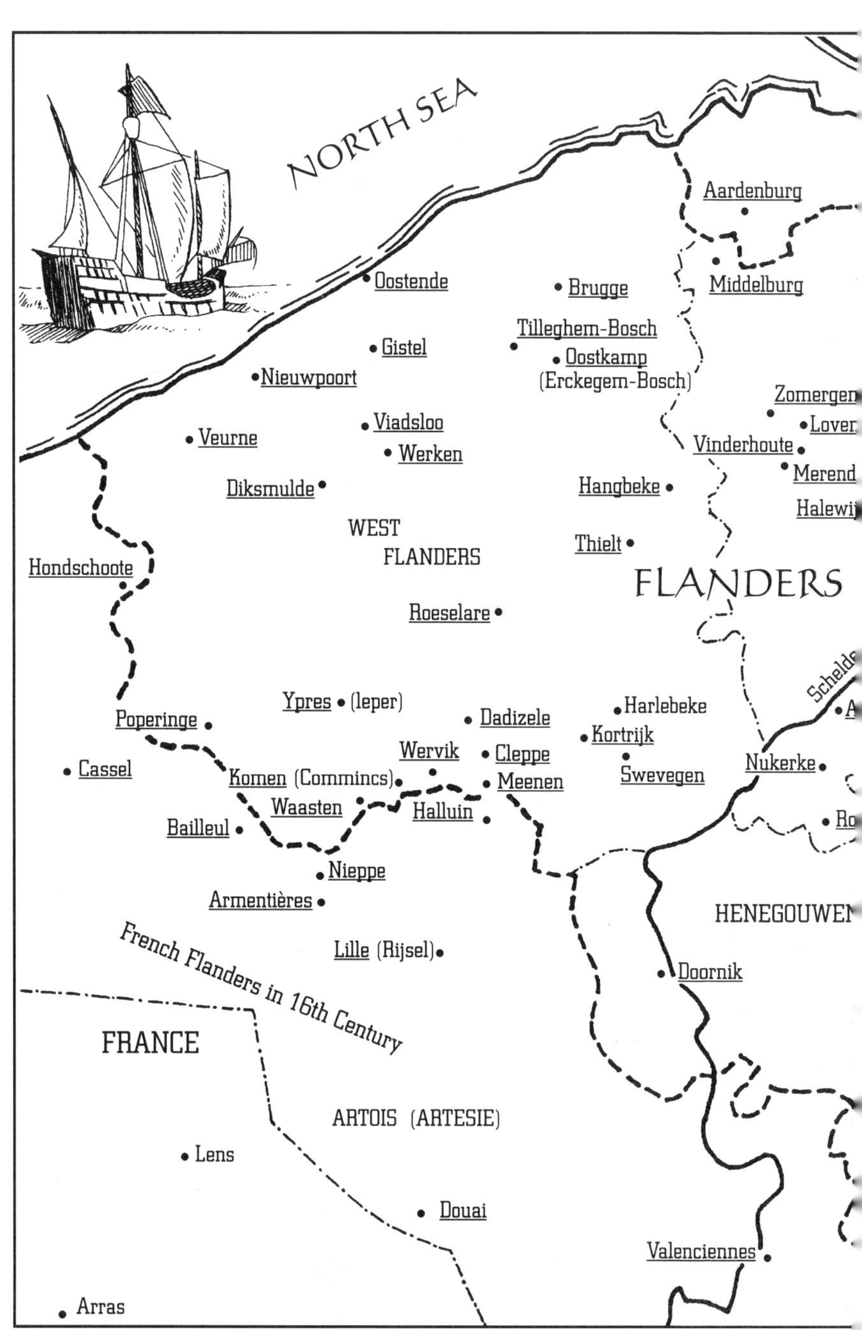
NORTH SEA
Aardenburg
Middelburg
Oostende
Brugge
Tilleghem-Bosch
Oostkamp
(Erckegem-Bosch)
Gistel
Nieuwpoort
Zomergem
Vinderhoute
Viadsloo
Werken
Veurne
Diksmulde
Hangbeke
WEST
FLANDERS
Thielt
Hondschoote
FLANDERS
Roeselare
Schelde
Ypres (Ieper)
Poperinge
Dadizele
Harlebeke
Kortrijk
Wervik
Cleppe
Swevegen
Nukerke
Cassel
Komen (Commincs)
Meenen
Waasten
Halluin
Bailleul
Nieppe
Armentières
HENEGOUWEN
Lille (Rijsel)
French Flanders in 16th Century
Doornik
FRANCE
ARTOIS (ARTESIE)
Lens
Douai
Valenciennes
Arras